THE

Dead

MOMS
CLUB

A MEMOIR

ABOUT DEATH, GRIEF,
AND SURVIVING THE
MOTHER OF ALL LOSSES

KATE SPENCER

SEAL PRESS

Seal Press
Hachette Book Group
1290 Avenue of the Americas, New York, NY 10104
www.SealPress.com
@SealPress

Printed in the United States of America

First Edition: November 2017

Published by Seal Press, an imprint of Perseus Books, LLC, a subsidiary of Hachette Book Group, Inc.

The publisher is not responsible for websites (or their content) that are not owned by the publisher.

"Motherf**kin' Mother's Day" was originally published on *Modern Loss* as "How I'm Making Mother's Day My Bitch."

"When the Grief Goes Away" was originally published on *BuzzFeed* as "How I Finally Let Go of Grief for My Dead Mom."

Yamada, Mitsuye. "What Your Mother Tells You." In *Camp Notes and Other Writings*, 1. New Brunswick: Rutgers University Press, 1998. Copyright © 1998 by Mitsuye Yamada. Reprinted by permission of Rutgers University Press.

Print book interior design by Jack Lenzo

Library of Congress Cataloging-in-Publication Data
Names: Spencer, Kate, 1979- author.
Title: The dead moms club : a memoir about death, grief, and surviving the mother of all losses / Kate Spencer.
Description: First Edition. | Boston : Seal Press, 2017. | Includes bibliographical references.
Identifiers: LCCN 2017037090| ISBN 9781580056878 (paperback) | ISBN 9781580056885 (ebook)
Subjects: LCSH: Children and death. | Mothers and daughters--Psychology. | Grief. | Loss (Psychology) | BISAC: BIOGRAPHY & AUTOBIOGRAPHY / Personal Memoirs.
Classification: LCC BF723.D3 .S645 2017 | DDC 155.9/37083--dc23
LC record available at https://lccn.loc.gov/2017037090

ISBNs: 978-1-58005-687-8 (paperback), 978-1-58005-688-5 (ebook)

LSC-C

10 9 8 7 6 5 4 3 2 1

Hello!

You're about to read a bunch of stories about the most difficult time in my life, told how I remember them. Some of the names and identifying specifics have been changed to maintain privacy, or because I'm a wuss and don't want to hurt people's feelings.

Also, there will be swearing. Sorry, Mom.

For Andrew

The Dead Moms Club
Meeting Agenda

———⟞⟝⟞⟝⟞———

Welcome

H i there. If you are reading this, it most likely means you are a member of one of the crappiest clubs in the world. I would love nothing more than to revoke my own membership to the Dead Moms Club and to turn you away at the door. To rip up our Dead Moms Club ID cards and throw them in an incinerator. But alas, once you're a member of this club, there's no way out. Also, I have no idea how to even find an incinerator, so we're definitely stuck.

(And if you're not a member of the Dead Moms Club yet, don't worry! Chances are you will be someday. And regardless, I've bet you've experienced deep loss and grief in your life, whether it be death, divorce, a pet passing away, or the end of *Six Feet Under*. The Babysitters Club had junior officers, members who were welcome but not quite at the level of Kristy, Claudia, Dawn, Stacey, and Mary Anne. That's what we'll call you.)

Remember how awful your stupid high school literary magazine club was? How insufferable every meeting felt? That's a walk in the park on a glorious spring day compared to this. I would sit through a lifetime of teenagers discussing their poems about the Beatles if it meant getting my mom back. But as we both know—*because, you know, our moms are dead*—life isn't fair sometimes. Also, poetry about the Beatles is almost certainly going to be awful. These are two things I know to be true.

No one asks to be enrolled in the Dead Moms Club, but since you're now a member, you deserve some support from someone who's been there. Someone who knows just how god-awful it is. Someone who's made it through.

That someone is me.

S ee, I'm not just the president of the Dead Moms Club. I'm also a client. Wait, no. That dated '90s joke doesn't quite work. But you get what I'm trying to say, right? I have a dead mom. I have been there and done *that*. I know just how bad it really is. I've been in the Club for a while.

My mom died when I was twenty-seven years old.* It was pancreatic cancer; it was fast; it was a nightmare. Just months before her diagnosis, she visited me at my tiny studio apartment in New York City. She slept on my couch, and we went shopping and split bottles of wine. Everything felt right. We were exactly where we needed to be in our relationship: true friends. When the weekend was over, I sent her off up Eighth Avenue, watching her walk toward Penn Station with her tiny

---

* It should be noted that up until this point my life had been a relative cakewalk, marked by the usual traumas that come when you're a mega-tall, shy extrovert who developed boobs in the fourth grade.

suitcase rolling at her side. The next time I saw her, she was in a hospital bed in Boston, cocooned in faded white sheets, a tumor hijacking her pancreas.

After her diagnosis I quit my production assistant job and moved home, back into my childhood bedroom. My younger brother, Andrew, did the same, and together with our father we served as my mother's caregivers until she died in the middle of an icy March night. We were huddled at her feet, sleeping around the hospital bed we had installed in my parents' bedroom. She took a few last sips of air, and then she left us.

Her illness and death transformed my life in extraordinary ways. It changed everything. For one hot second there I even entertained the idea of becoming a social worker, because my life felt so completely meaningless. But then I realized I would make a terrible social worker, and I snapped out of it, sticking to the stable, lucrative career of writer and comedian instead. It's what my mom would have wanted.

Knowing my mom, she'd probably also have wanted me to turn my grief into something more than just a pyramid of snot-soaked tissues.* Because let me tell you, when it comes to gut-stabbing, endless sadness—the kind that feels like a Chuck E. Cheese's ball pit that you can't seem to climb out of—I have been there. I've logged my ten thousand hours of weeping, making me a Malcolm Gladwell–approved genius at sobbing into an Ikea couch pillow. I have fallen into the deepest of lows—horrible, dark places from which I thought I'd

---

* Though, come to think of it, that would be *very* impressive and probably result in instant D-list celebrity status and a lifetime of free Kleenex. Hmmmmm. *Adds tissue pyramid to to-do list.*

never escape. And yet here I am, typing these words right now to you. I am even wearing actual pants, so you know I'm doing all right. (Okay fine, they're leggings. But still.)

I made it through. I have lived through the loss of my mom and survived, and you can, too. Do I still have unstoppable bouts of crying after watching *Stepmom*? Of course, I'm only human. Everyone needs a good Susan-Sarandon-and-Julia-Roberts-inspired sob fest every now and then. But still, I'm functioning. I'm making it. And that's what I am here to tell you. *You got this.*

The Dead Moms Club is my story of dealing with my own grief, as well as all the weird, unexpected things that came along with it. (Disordered eating! Who knew?) I can only venture to speak to my own experience, since I've only had and lost my mom, Martha Spencer, amazing listener, occasional grudge-holder, lover of *Days of Our Lives* and Oprah Winfrey, proud feminist, and caring human who bought birthday cards in bulk so she'd always have one to send. Good Lord, I miss her.

Still, despite our different moms and experiences, this is also a book of commiseration, support, and the occasional survival tip on how to make it as a member of the Dead Moms Club. Through telling my own story of loss, I hope to help you get through yours, too. Or at least make you feel a little less alone. Because no matter how varied our experiences may be, we can all agree that losing your mom sucks, right? *RIGHT?*

Most importantly, this book is a safe space for you to grieve in whatever way you want. Read a page, put it down, and come back to it when you're ready. Devour the whole thing in one night. Let it sit on a shelf for years, or use it as a coaster until

you're ready to give it a read. Kill a cockroach with it. Whatever you need, I'm here.

Now, hold these.

[*Hands you a giant glass of your drink of choice, a bowl of*
the saltiest potato chips imaginable, and a Snickers bar the size
of a pillow.]

See, the first rule of the Dead Moms Club is that you
may stuff your face with whatever the hell you want, whenever you want. If you want fruit, it's in the fridge behind the
endless supply of brie cheese. Gluten-free bagels are in the
bread drawer next to the gluten-full loaves. The Nutella is
in the bathtub. Yes, that's what that tub full of brown stuff
is. Come on, what did you expect? Grieving takes up a lot of
energy. You're gonna need it. Also, please blow your nose and
wipe your tears on whatever you want around here. That's the
second rule of the Dead Moms Club. Because after all, this is
a safe space (for cry-snot, especially).

The third rule: grieving is best when done however *you*
want to do it. It's up to you—and only you—how you get
through this.

Rule number four: take all the time you need.

And the fifth and final rule of the Dead Moms Club?
You're totally allowed to side-eye all people who say, "At least
she's in a better place now." Screw them.

Welcome. I'm so sorry you're here.

2

She's Dead.
So Now What?

My mom died at 2:04 AM on your average March night in Massachusetts: bleak, black, and so cold that the air freezes your snot to the walls of your nose the second you step outside. On her last night on earth, my dad, my brother, Andrew, and I slept at her feet like dogs, loyal and desperate for her love and affection until the very end. We had started hospice at our house a mere two weeks prior, but it felt as if I'd been doing it since birth. We were living on animal instincts alone: eat some lasagna; administer an extremely high dose of morphine; cry hysterically; return to administer an extremely high dose of Haldol; eat more lasagna; chug a bottle of wine; refresh Mom's water; finish the lasagna. Repeat.

When we started hospice, we were all naively hopeful it would give us a few more months together. "I just want her to live long enough to hear the birds in spring," my dad said wistfully as we washed dishes together one night. My mom was asleep upstairs in her new-spangled hospital bed. This is the true sign that someone is nearing death: the closer they get to the end of their life, the more your house fills up with items straight out of a medical catalog.

First it had been the shower chair. "Just one last thing to worry about!" we'd said with a forced excitement that comes with caregiver territory. But then came the toilet chair ("Less bending over!" we'd cheered), and the walker ("So much safer!"), and the strange, smaller items, like the tiny mouth-swab sticks that we were constantly dipping into cups of water and smudging against my mom's gums to keep her hydrated when she became a comatose shell of herself.

Soon our house was chock full of these gray, plastic, sterile contraptions, a wall-to-wall reminder that "Someone Is Dying Here." But nothing signals that the Grim Reaper is on his way like the arrival of the hospital bed. If a house with a terminal cancer patient is a museum of death-support tools, the hospital bed is the *Mona Lisa*, the pièce de résistance.

There had been no miracles for my mom. She had terrible reactions to the first chemo regimen she tried—a strange red rash that made her skin look like the outside of a strawberry—and it did nothing to stop the spots on her liver from spreading. The second chemo kept everything stable for a couple months as summer shifted to fall, willing us to get sucked into the magical feeling that is Hope. But it was short-lived; come November, a sepsis infection caused her gallbladder to collapse, and the whole ordeal sucked the pounds off her body like liposuction gone comically wrong. Her hair went from full and dark to thin and gray. Her transformation into shriveled old lady happened almost overnight, and she returned home from the hospital with tubes draining bile from her stomach, too weak to continue with chemo.

But hospice. This would be the thing to keep her alive! *Hospice.* The word even sounds soft and cozy, a promising whisper on your lips. I felt giddy about it. *Hey, we may not get to keep her forever,* I reasoned, *but hospice will give us some months to soak up each other's essence, to swap life lessons and stories, to marvel at the circle of life as spring blossoms around us.* I was high on my own denial, trying to haggle cancer into letting us keep her around for just a little bit longer. *Maybe,* I thought to myself, *she'll even make it to summer! We can just go on and on like this, keeping her barely alive and showering in a gray plastic chair from season to season.*

Sometimes it's hard to see through your sorrow at just how much illness and death changes your life. "This is all totally normal!" you sing, twirling on your mountaintop of hospital stuff like Maria in *The Sound of Music.* But then you blink, and you see it: nothing is normal. Your parents' queen-size bed is gone, shoved into a corner of the basement. Your mom's bed-side table, once home to a precariously stacked collection of Sue Grafton mysteries, is now just a forest of pill bottles and cups of ice water. Your dad sleeps on a cot on the floor. You and your brother curl up in a pile of blankets at the foot of the hospital bed, waking at four AM to douse your shell of a mother with morphine. You deliver each dose through tears, panicked that the pain meds might kill her before the cancer does.

This time when life crosses into death is dark and raw and, frankly, terrifying to revisit. Ten years later, and it is still one gray blur of the deepest, most bone-crushing sadness I have

ever known. I can still feel the despair pouring out of me, like
some sort of viral illness. And the memories are tinged with
shame, because I so desperately just wanted her to die during
the last week of her life. I wanted this awful misery trapping
my family to be over, wanted my mom's suffering to stop. But I
also hated what the cancer did to her. It stole her away, sucked
the life out of her—her body tossed aside, an empty cup. In
those last two weeks of her life, she was gone but still alive.
She was not actually dead yet; she could moan, and breathe,
and sleep. But the woman who'd sometimes still climbed in
bed with me to sing lullabies, even though I was long out of
college, was gone. The woman who'd bought thirty air fresh-
eners at the hardware store "just in case," even though we only
needed one, was gone. The woman I'd watched cook dinner
with the phone tucked under her chin, laughing to a friend as
the endless, curly phone cord wrapped slowly around her waist
as she moved, was gone. Just like that.

My mom had left the building, but her body was still there.

I did not like the creature left in her place. She was zombie-
like, her eyes stuck half-open, her mouth ajar, her breath rattling in her chest like a tiny Salvation Army bell ringer. If you
have been through this purgatory of They're Not Dead Yet
but, Holy Crap, They Sure Aren't Alive Either, you know what
I'm talking about. (If you haven't, that means your mom died
another different but equally awful way, and I am so very sorry.)

With the arrival of this Zombie Mom, I stopped sobbing
desperate pleas of "please let my mom live" into my pillow at
night. Now, I desperately wanted her to die, for her body to
join the rest of her, far away from this misery.

When you start hospice, someone—a nurse in white clogs, or your social worker in her bejeweled glasses—will hand you a little blue booklet with a crude drawing of a boat on it. Receiving this book, *Gone from My Sight*, is a rite of passage, like some sort of induction ritual into a death sorority. It is the *What to Expect When You're Expecting* of dying, detailing what will go down the closer your loved one gets to death. There's the way the body can be both bony and swollen, the limbs blue. There's the death rattle, that terrible name for the short, violent, fluid-filled, end-of-life breath. And then there's terminal agitation, when the dying person can suddenly become delirious, confused, and restless, with bouts of strength and energy. And it is, simply, awful to witness.

One night, she tried to escape. For days she'd been muttering "I've got to go," while constantly trying to get up and down out of her bed. She demanded we change her shirt, all day, over and over again. I was sitting next to her on the edge of the mattress during one of the wardrobe changes when she suddenly jerked upward. With the strength of a thousand Olympic sprinters, my mom, who had previously needed help to walk to the bathroom just steps from her bed, stood up and ran into my bedroom, climbing into my bed. "I've got to go!" she shouted at me. I screamed to my dad for help, and he charged up the stairs, my brother close behind. Somehow he managed to calm her down, moving her out of my bed and back toward her room. She stopped in front of the bathroom in the hallway. "I need to pee," she insisted, even though there was barely any liquid left in her body. She was leaning on my dad now, her strength gone just as quickly as it arrived. As he lowered her onto the toilet, she put her hands to her head, moaning. "What's happening to me?" she whimpered softly. "Am I dying?"

"Yes," he said, his voice cracking. "I think so, and it's okay." The three of us began our 8,683,596th bout of ugly sobbing as we stood in a semicircle around her. Our hospice nurse had instructed us to give her permission to go, let her know we were okay with her leaving us. But the words still sounded crazy. "You can die," he assured her over and over again. "You can die."

But she didn't. That night, her rambling continued. "Goodbye, good night," she said, over and over again, tucked into her bed. "I've got to go." Then she told each one of us that she loved us and demanded we leave her room. "Just go," she said.

The three of us got to the bottom of the stairs and collapsed as one blubbering conglomerate on the stiff, pristine black couch in our living room, the one we only sat on during Christmas. The three of us so worn down by cancer despite our bodies being totally fine. When the tears let up, we wandered into the kitchen, unsure of how to proceed. Do we go upstairs? Do we give her space to die? No one knew what to do, so we did the logical thing and got slightly drunk while watching *American Idol*. When we finally went back upstairs, she was still there, breathing.

She lived for five more days.

G rowing up, when the humid swell of July reached its sticky, miserable peak, my friends and I would fill water balloons and hurl them at each other. We lived in an ancient time before Minecraft and YouTube stars, and we could only watch *You Can't Do That on Television* so many times before we started to get antsy. We'd stomp into the house in our jelly shoes and our jelly bracelets (the '80s: a terrible time for fashion, a great time for jelly), balloons in hand, and yank their bright, rubber mouths up and around the kitchen faucet, filling them with water until they bulged, their skins stretched. They'd be so full we could barely tie them, our fingers getting tangled in the middle of the knots as we scrambled to secure our weapons. The balloons were huge in our hands, until that sweet, satisfying moment when they hit the ground, dissolving into shreds of blue, green, and red in an instant.

This is how it is when death finally comes. Your fear, anxiety, and sorrow stretch and expand, but you make room for the pain in ways you never thought possible. And then suddenly, it all hits, explodes, and you are decimated. Soaked in it. And there is nothing normal about what follows: the quiet in your house, the shifting of schedules to adopt all the things she once did, the cold, gray hospital toilet chair, now collecting dust upstairs.

The weeks that follow stretch on forever, like those minutes you spend waiting for a first date to show up at your house. You create chores for yourself, fill the time cleaning out Tupperware drawers or examining the strange cans of things your mom left in her obsessively overstocked pantry. I would stand with the door open, weeping at the site of can after can of Jolly Green Giant peas, angry that I now had no one at whom to yell, "Girl, why the hell do you have all these gross peas?"

A couple weeks after we buried her in a cheap, wooden urn in the rock-hard New Hampshire ground, a massive snowstorm hit New England. We're talking two feet of thick, wet snow blanketing everything in sight. The kind of snow that sneaks into your boots even if your boots come up to your shoulders. The kind of snow everyone who grows up in Southern California dreams of experiencing, only to be completely horrified the first time they live through it. The kind of snow that eats up the world around it, like a fungus. *New England snow.*

It was April, or as we Yanks like to call it: The Month When Spring Is Supposed to Start But Instead We Just Got Two Feet of Snow. The blizzard had finally stopped, and it was a terrible time to hit the roads. They were slick and icy, and hardly plowed. But I was headed back to New York City soon, marking the official end of my nine-month-long Dying Mom Sabbatical. This would be my last time in a while to "see" her. And so my dad and I hopped in his four-wheel-drive-less sedan, flipped the seat warmers on, and headed off, swerving our way along the not-quite-plowed streets to the cemetery.

She was buried on top of a hill overlooking the green, sloping hills of southern New Hampshire, just a few steps south of her own mom's granite headstone. This was her hometown, the place of her birth and childhood. My parents owned a second home just down the road; it was where they'd planned on living after retirement. Now she was getting an early start.

It was a beautiful spot, but one you had to gun your car up a fairly steep hill to get to. She'd only been buried for a few weeks, and so she had no headstone yet, just a small marker stuck in the ground noting her burial spot. Now it was

completely covered in snow. Wait, did I mention everything
was covered in hard, wet snow? I did? Let me say it again:
THERE WAS SNOW. *EVERYWHERE.*

But nothing could stop us. We were sad warriors, determined and on a mission to be . . . more sad! Besides, we had
already vacuumed the house, like, fifty times. We needed an
activity to keep us busy, and our favorite hobby was grieving.
Who cared if the dude on NPR was encouraging people to
stay off the roads because of the ice? Off we charged into battle, weather be damned. For as the old song goes: *You gotta
fight! For your right! To awkwardly cry with your dad in front of
your mom's new graveeeeeeee!*

The place was packed with other families who had braved
the snow to mourn their loved ones. Nope, just kidding—it
was empty and silent and dead like the people who occupied
its tombs, because the rest of the world was a hundred times
smarter than we were and reserved their public displays of
grief for days with better weather. The tombstones around us
might as well have read: Here Lies Joe Smith. His Family Is
Sane and Only Visits When It's Above 40 Degrees Outside.

"I don't know about this," I said as we passed under the
large stone-and-iron gate that welcomed visitors into the most
depressing place on earth.

"Kate," my dad said confidently, his voice laced with the
smugness of someone who'd driven this cemetery road a lot in
the past two weeks. "We'll be fine."

Undeterred, he wove the car along the road, which curved
by the older tombstones that seemed to be sinking into the
earth, with dates like 1836 carved on the top. He blasted the
gas as we hit the bottom of the hill, and the car began to fly up

the road. *Mom!* I cheered to myself. *We're coming! We're almost there! We're—*

We're stuck.

The tires whirred against the ice and gravel, but our car was firmly stuck in place on the road, about three-quarters of the way up the hill.

"It's fine," my dad said, sensing my immediate judgment.

"We can just turn around," I suggested, unconvinced. "Or reverse down the hill?"

"No, no, if I just . . . " My dad shifted gears and stepped on the gas. We didn't move.

He tried this for five minutes, gunning and stopping and turning, gunning and stopping and turning, until he eventually sighed in defeat. "We're not going anywhere," he said.

"You think?" I agreed, forever the family know-it-all.

He shifted the car in reverse to back down the hill, per my original, brilliant plan. We slid slowly, evenly until—"Goddamn it!" The car shifted sideways into the snowbank behind us. Somehow the car had twisted itself at an angle, splayed out across the road like a diagonal win in a game of tic-tac-toe.

"Well, this can't be good," I snorted, because in addition to being a know-it-all, I am also a snarky asshole. My dad glared at me through his bifocals. He tried to slowly do a fifty-two-point turn on the road but just kept getting the car more and more wedged between the walls of snow that bordered the road like some sort of *Game of Thrones* hellscape. "Call your brother," he growled at me. "And tell him to bring a shovel."

As we waited for Andrew to arrive, my dad attempted to stomp the rest of the way up the hill toward my mom. He first tried just to walk up the road, slowly placing one foot ahead of the other. But it quickly became clear that the ice beneath his feet was working against him, sliding him back down the hill with every step, like a kid walking the wrong way on one of those people-moving walkways at the airport. Plan B: he straddled the snowbank and heaved himself into the snow. On paper this was a logical plan: he'd walk through the graves to where my mom lay a hundred feet north of him. But snow makes every pragmatic idea real stupid, real fast. He pounded his foot down, and suddenly he was up to his knees in powder; he could barely lift his leg out to propel the other one forward. What would be a two-minute huff up a hill in the summer now felt like a trek up Everest. He turned back around, defeated.

My mom was so close, but the snow made it feel as if she were a million miles away. Which she *was*. She was everywhere and nowhere. She was just up the hill, but she was also gone. Completely gone.

Fifteen minutes later, my brother's car peeled in under the gate and sped toward us up the hill. And from about twenty yards away we heard the familiar whir of tires spinning against gravel and ice.

He was stuck, too.

"Goddamn it," my dad said again, but this time he was laughing. My brother leapt out, lifting his hands in defeat. He had driven over expecting to simply drop off a shovel and head back home, and he was not dressed for winter rescue. He popped open the trunk of the car, grabbing the requested shovels, while Dad retrieved a couple of ice scrapers from his trunk. The three of us got to work digging out both cars, chipping away at the snowbanks so we'd have room to turn both cars around. We dug and picked and scraped with fury as my mom watched from her icy perch above us. Sad warriors, defeated. It was the first time since her death that the four of us had been together—just the four of us. Misshapen, beaten down, and different, but a family, still.

In those early days, the grief was overwhelming and all-consuming, a black hole sucking everything away so that nothing was left but hot, swirling pain. It was all I could think about, like a middle school crush. I woke up consumed by my mom's absence, moved through the world hypnotized by it, then fell asleep to the lullaby of my tears. I was desperate to encounter her in my dreams, but my sleep was heavy, empty, and dark—proof that there really was no getting her back.

I thought about her during every single interaction. The more boring and mundane it was, the more I felt her death hovering over me.

"Would you like room in your coffee for cream?"

"My mom is dead and never coming back, so yes. Yes, I do."

The terrifying thing about grief is how easy it can be to function in your day-to-day life while it quietly eats away at you. As the days turned into weeks and, suddenly, months, I lugged my grief around with me like a shiny new purse, bringing it everywhere I went.

Two months after my mom died, I landed my dream job—off a Craigslist ad, no less—writing about celebrities and pop culture at VH1. It was a perfect match for my interests (the comings and goings of Lindsay Lohan, and not much else), and my unconditionally supportive mom would have been thrilled for me. But with every step I took to the subway, every swipe of my ID card to enter my office lobby, my grief was there, throbbing in my bones and muscle and skin. My body felt as if it had taken twenty-four hours of spin classes, but without the actual abs to show for it. I ached. My grief leaked out of every orifice of my body no matter what I did to try to clog it, keep it down, and shove it inside.

I waffled between being unable to even say the words "my mom died" to then wanting to talk about nothing else but my dead mom. Somehow both emotions existed inside me and could change rank on the minute. And it was always all or nothing: I was either dead silent or fighting the urge to climb to the tops of mountains (or even just a chair at Starbucks) and scream, "MY MOM IS DEAD!!!!" On those days I wanted to saturate the world in my grief, so that maybe someone could understand just how bad I felt.

Often, when people would ask how I was doing, I'd simply reply, "Not great, my mom just died." This is a terrible way to make friends, but my grief had ushered all social norms out of the room. Saying the words helped because I couldn't quite believe it, and saying it out loud reminded me that it was real. But there was a deeper, darker, meaner part of me that liked seeing people squirm. Maybe if I made enough people uncomfortable, I could somehow get them to feel my pain. And so there it sat on my tongue, ready to leap out at strangers any chance it got.

On one of my first days at VH1 I went with some coworkers to grab an afternoon coffee, the three of us weaving through the sweaty crowds of Times Square in a single line. We small-talked during whatever pocket of silence we could find, and as we were riding the elevator back to our floor, one of them turned to me, her hands full of giant white cups. "So what were you doing before this?" she asked politely with a smile. It was an innocuous question, one that I could have answered by listing some of my writing bylines in a couple of seconds. Instead, I dropped this charmer: "Oh, I moved home to take care of my mom after she got diagnosed with cancer."

Everyone in the elevator grew suddenly stiff, like someone had just ripped the worst-smelling fart imaginable. My coffee cup seemed comically large in my hands.

Somewhere along the way I'd lost sight of the fact that, despite it being my norm, dead moms were not something most people mentioned casually. And really, I wasn't trying to be morbid. In the moment, I simply didn't want her to think that my lack of recent work was because of some glaring, unemployable flaw.

"Wow," she responded, stunned, her voice lower. "Is she . . . okay?"

"No, she died, like, two months ago," I said casually, as if I were discussing the socks I just bought at Target. I had no idea how people talked about the very sad things in their lives. But also, embarrassingly, I was trying to be nonchalant and cool. *Everyone loves a cool girl*, I reasoned. *They'll love one who's super down and chill with having a dead mom!*

We rode the rest of the way in silence.

M y mom and I had only transitioned into the friendship phase of our relationship a few years before she got sick. Gone were the antagonistic teen years, when I hid vodka in Poland Spring water bottles, and she found said water bottles and yelled at me for stealing from the liquor cabinet and drinking while underage, and I yelled back about her snooping through my stuff. I had been the kind of kid who, after a fight, once ripped up a picture of my mom and me, right down the middle, and left it outside her bedroom door. I was a brooder, certain I was misunderstood by everyone except my faceless online friends. To make matters worse, I was deep into my Grateful Dead and Phish phase, and wore terrible homemade patchwork clothes that I cobbled together on my mom's old sewing machine. These screaming fights took place while I was dressed like a clown from a 1970s PBS children's show. I was the worst kind of teenage hippie. You know the one, who insists their mom cook vegetarian meals for the whole family and then sneaks slices of salami when no one's looking. In hindsight, she had good reason to be perpetually irritated with me.

When I hit my early twenties, we transitioned into a space of mutual love, understanding, and trust. I got older and matured, she eased up and relaxed, and a true friendship blossomed. I took out my eyebrow and nose rings, which I know secretly pleased her. But I also lost the resentment I'd built up as a teenager, and the screaming fights we'd had in the parking lot of Bed Bath & Beyond the summer before I left for college were now a distant memory.

Despite our differences, we always genuinely liked each other, with shared affection for people watching, Dansko clogs, and self-deprecating humor. But in my twenties, we started to feel like actual friends, and our battles during my teen years were now simply the stuff of legend, laughed about over dinners out with my brother and dad. I relished her visits to New

York City: the sleepovers in my shoebox apartment and the endless avocado toast and bra shopping. (You never can have enough mother-daughter bra shopping, you know?) I imagined we'd go on like this for years, maybe travel the world sampling avocado toasts in cities around America. Eventually I'd have kids, and we'd bring them along, too, make it a whole tradition. The way some people map out lives with their lovers, I envisioned a future with my mom: one of hearty laughs, chatty dinners, and holding hands exploring cobblestone streets packed with quaint storefronts and twee art museums.

Then suddenly, the cancer apocalypse hit, and a dizzying nine months later, she was dead. I was twenty-seven years old, in the thick of that wonderfully selfish midtwenties time when I was supposed to be figuring out who I was and exploring all avenues of my adult self, like staying out drinking until two AM and still making it to work by eight. Instead I was consumed with my sorrow and loss, and my grief shifted from a coping mechanism to my whole identity.

My brother and father were also deep in the trenches of grief, but in those first few months I was too absorbed in my own pain to even begin to acknowledge theirs. We'd always been a close family and bonded even more as my mom's caregivers, but now we were scattered up and down the East Coast, mourning on our own. They threw themselves into new adventures: my brother started business school in North Carolina; my dad went back to work and learned how to cook dinner for himself (aka he went to the deli counter at Roche Bros. after work). My relationships—with my fiancé, friends, and colleagues—quickly became an afterthought, my hobbies nonexistent. They were no match for the constant sadness that scrolled through me like a news ticker, distracting me from focusing on what was happening directly in front of me.

I spent most of my time in my apartment, four flights up in the sky on a Chelsea street, wallowing. I cheated on my boy-friend-turned-fiancé (turned husband!), Anthony, with my self-pity. Every night I'd come home from work and sit on my bed, digging through the pretty, apple-green Container Store box I'd purchased to hold things that reminded me of her: handwrit-ten notes, old birthday cards, the hospital bracelets I'd saved without telling her. I read and reread old emails, the most mundane correspondences shaking me the most. "So maybe your gas issue is realted [*sic*] to gluten allergy," she wrote, offer-ing me advice about a rash in February 2006. "It means not eating lots of what you like. It is hard."

(For what it's worth my "gas issue" was not a gluten allergy. I'm just gross.)

Nothing made her feel more alive again than when she was at her most nagging. "Kate," she instructed on a yellow Post-it. "You have to fill out the customer agreement & the assumption of liability form. Then return to Verizon. They did not include an envelope. xoxo Mom."

Just looking at her scribbled signature could launch her back to life to the point where I could almost trick myself into believing she was still alive. Revisiting that deep, endless sad-ness again and again allowed me to remember all the details about her I feared I might forget, to touch and smell and see her. I began to not just enjoy these daily grieving rituals but crave them. Nowhere in the five stages of grief does Elisabeth

Kübler-Ross mention that mourning might actually feel good. I was happy existing in a perpetual state of grief because it kept my mom alive.

W hen you lose someone you love, the phrase "new normal" gets thrown around a lot. As if you just need to adjust to this new, gaping life wound and then everything else will simply stabilize and the world will go on, slightly different from how it was before. Let us all please gather in a circle and give this phrase the middle finger, shall we? Because seriously, screw your new normal. First of all, my life before my mom died was anything but normal.* And second, our lives aren't something to be divvied up into neat Before and After slices, like pie. That, readers, is simply not how it works.

You have one, long, messy, weird, beautiful life. People come in and out of it, live and die, and affect us in enormous— or not so enormous—ways. Your mom's death is now a piece of you, a new dent on the side of the strange, misshapen thing that is your life.

I grew up spending summers with my extended family on a tiny lake in New Hampshire, which was as idyllic as it sounds. (I am very lucky.) My cousins and I hunted for salamanders with our bare hands and swung on hammocks for hours on end, sandwiched next to each other like graham crackers stacked neatly in their package. Each summer, we'd wade

---

* In the seventh grade I bet my best friend twenty-five cents that she couldn't poop in her pants on cue, and I lost. I've been weird forever—sorry.

into the water and build rock towers along the edge, where the pine-needle-covered earth sinks into the cool, dark lake. Even now this tradition continues, and by the end of August the small beach is full, stones on top of stones, balancing there as the seasons change around them until they eventually fall. I like to think of our lives this way; we start with one stone at the bottom and slowly build upwards, experiences and moments balancing precariously on top of each other, making up who we are. And when the elements knock the rocks over, we rebuild, with the same pieces but a new shape. We are different, misshapen and unsteady, but still whole. Still standing.

Surviving your motherless world is not something you can take day by day, or hour by hour. It is smaller, way more minuscule than that. It's like the world's smallest baby taking the tiniest baby steps imaginable. You get through it breath by painful breath. It's literally that slow, that incremental. It feels like nothing is changing—until suddenly it is.

Now hey, you may be fine. You may soar through your grief with the ease of Bette Midler singing "Wind Beneath My Wings." And if you do, Godspeed, my sweet angel! You have figured it all out and are a sentient being worthy of eternal adoration.

But the rest of us will plod, stumble, and flail. We will weep like no one's watching. We will numb ourselves with things that may or may not be healthy. Our grief will trap us like one of those Escape the Room games our coworkers swear will be fun.

You will not know *how* you're going to make it through, and yet you will. *You will.* Because I say so, and I am a lady who wrote a book about grief, so I know things.*

⸻ ❧ ⸻

THINGS YOU DEFINITELY DON'T NEED TO WORRY ABOUT RIGHT AFTER YOUR MOM DIES

- Showering.
- Washing your face.
- Shaving.
- Just, like, any basic exterior body upkeep whatsoever. Just make sure you wipe when you go to the bathroom.
- Getting dressed.
- Eating well.
- Exercise.
- Returning emails.
- Or phone calls.
- Or texts.
- Or Instagram DMs.
- Writing thank-you notes. Maybe someday. Not now.
- Drinking sixty-four ounces of water a day.

_____

* All I really know is that Cheez-Its are the best snack. That's it. But it's something, right?

- Meditating.
- Journaling.
- Making it to yoga class.
- Committing to that Whole30 diet you've been meaning to try.
- Making sense in conversations.
- Taking your vitamins.
- Updating your résumé.
- Knowing what people are talking about in pop culture.
- Politics.
- Recycling. (Go ahead and throw that plastic takeout container in the trash. I won't tell.)
- Your vision board.
- Life goals.
- Career goals.
- Finishing *The Goldfinch*.
- Quitting coffee.

THINGS YOU DEFINITELY DO NEED TO WORRY ABOUT RIGHT AFTER YOUR MOM DIES

- Feeding yourself whatever you can stomach eating. Chocolate counts.
- Hydrating enough so you don't faint.
- Being gentle and kind toward yourself, and your grief.
- Being gentle and kind toward those who are grieving along with you.

- Making sure your bills are paid so you don't end up without electricity or internet. (Grieving without access to Netflix is a criminal offense.)
- Taking care of the people or animals for whom you are responsible.
- Sleeping whenever you can.
- Changing your underwear. Occasionally.

3

Breaking the News

Life goes on after your mom dies. Not eventually. Like, the same day. One minute you are watching as paramedics lug your mother's body out of her bedroom in a black body bag, blowing tears out of your nose and snot out of your eyes. Then, an hour later, you are bent over outside in your now-dead mom's bright orange winter coat (the one she'd wear on purpose to your soccer games because she knew you hated it), your fingers freezing as they press against the inside of a plastic bag, prying dog crap off of the frozen ground. Dogs still have to go to the bathroom after people die, and while animals are intuitive, they're not smart enough to sense that they should hold it in for a few years while you take the world's longest, tear-filled shower.

It's hard enough that the Worst Thing in the World just happened and you still have to brush your teeth, put on clothes, and try to eat. But someone also has to tell everyone in the world that she's gone. That someone is *you*, and boy, nothing rubs salt in the Dead Mom Wound like having to tell people over and over again that she's dead.

Hours after my mom's body was loaded into the funeral home's hearse, I sat at her desk in our kitchen, working my way through a list of names she'd scribbled out when still alive. My dad and I split them up to tackle together—he handled our family, and I got her friends. Unfortunately, despite our entire lives now being captured on Snapchat or typed out with emojis, dropping the Dead Mom Bomb is still a thing best done by using your actual, human voice. Our script went like this:

"Hi [insert name here: her trainer-turned-friend, her best friend who lived down the street and selected her as godmother to her son, the first friend she made at college], I'm calling to tell you that my mom passed away last night. We were all with her, around her bed. Around two AM. It was peaceful. Yeah, I'm just glad she's no longer in pain. We're doing okay. My dad's okay, thanks. I'm okay. Yup, Andrew's doing okay. We did get your lasagna/card/flowers, thanks so much. Okay, okay. Thanks. I'll definitely call if we need something."

It's horrible news to deliver, even when expected, and the conversation that ensues will be the most awkward one of your life—until you call the next person on your list. The person on the other end of the phone is grappling with grief, helplessness, and an urge to help you, while you've got your own grief and helplessness going on compounded by an urge to help *them*. It's a mess.

The people on our call lists were a big part of our family's life: friends who brought broccoli salad to summer barbecues and relatives who were overly supportive during my terrible teen phases, like when I showed up to Thanksgiving one year with my eyebrow freshly pierced. The interactions were occasionally awkward (has there ever been a nonawkward "I'm calling to tell you someone is dead" conversation?) but not unexpected, so I became relatively confident in handling the conversations and the emotions that followed. You cry; they cry. You blow your nose too loudly in the receiver, they laugh at the joke you make about it after. And then you hang up.

But no one prepares you for how to tell the *other* people in your life: your mechanic, the overly friendly checkout lady at Shaw's, the mailman who once accidentally dropped off your college acceptance letter at the wrong house. Our worlds are so much bigger than just friends and family, and the people who exist on the outer perimeter often care about us just as much as our closest friends. The mechanic and my mom yukked it up every year during her car inspection; the checkout lady knew her birthday; the mailman opened up about his own battle with pancreatitis when he learned about her cancer. They all loved my mother—an outgoing introvert who claimed shyness but was warm and open to everyone. They *knew* her, and now they needed to know that she was gone.

The dog groomer was one of those people.

Just a few days after my mom died, I shoved my body into whatever clothes were on my bedroom floor and drove my parents' Jeep Grand Cherokee to the groomer. You'd think that I'd want to curl up inside my childhood bed and never leave the house, but I was desperate to get out of there. I was in a dead-mom-induced daze, and I needed something to do. My mom had been the Thing for nine straight months—she'd filled my days with protein shakes to make, Oxycontins to dole out, doctors to visit, fevers to fret about, and laxatives to buy. The anxiety her cancer caused was endless and all-consuming, but it was *something*. Now all that work was over, and my days were empty and open, filled only with a deep, painful longing—for her, for our life before cancer, for anything else but this new, motherless world.

Simon, our ten-pound Maltese terrier, was the kind of dog you tolerated instead of liked, a pet store purchase made after months of relentless begging when I was twelve.* I discovered him during our weekly trips to Debby's Petland to buy live crickets and mealworms for the tiny green lizard I convinced my mom I had to have and then promptly ignored the second he moved home with us. I was the last person on earth who deserved another pet. We already had one dog—a basset hound named Lucy who smelled like a gym bag left in the back of your trunk for too long in July. And I had a terrible animal track record: in addition to the lizard, I once brought home a rabbit who promptly ate the new molding in our sunroom, and then gave birth to a bunch of babies and *ate them*. Yet somehow I manipulated my mom into welcoming another disaster of an animal into our home.

Simon began snarling and trying to bite off chunks of people's bodies just a few months after we got him, which set off years of visits to the vet, obedience trainers, and animal psychologists. We tried Prozac, which did nothing to help his behavioral problems but was great at getting him to have diarrhea all over the kitchen. One doctor suggested a food allergy might be making him irritable, so my mom prepared him elaborate meals made of organic ground lamb and rice, while we ate chicken nuggets cooked in the toaster oven. He'd come home from visits to the groomer and stays at the kennel with

---

* Please only adopt animals from shelters and rescues. Thank you.

an F on his dog report card, which is a thing those places hand out to make owners feel like garbage about how they're failing their animal children. Eventually we just forced Simon to march around our house dragging a tiny blue leash behind him. We'd stomp on the leash just when he was about to trap someone in his mouth, saving the day and their skin.

My mom was his main caregiver, partially because she was stuck with the job when I escaped to college, but also because she was the only person in the house who was nice to the little asshole. They had an understanding and a bond, and he'd grown noticeably subdued as her health deteriorated, pacing around the bottom of the staircase as she lay dying in her bedroom above. Even though he had the warmth of a dictator, he still had a heart, and it was clear her death had softened him. I almost started to feel bad for him, this poor little dog who had lost his most treasured human. We had that in common, at least. Maybe we could learn to love each other through our pain. But then he bared his teeth at me because I dared to sit next to him on the couch, and I went right back to hating him without shame.

I was raised by the kind of responsible human who scheduled appointments out a year in advance, so Simon hit up the groomer every six weeks, like clockwork. I'd assumed the drop-off duty since moving back home and had barely exchanged more than a "Hello, I'm sorry our dog has the personality of a land mine" with the groomer the entire time. But she'd clearly caught on that my mom was no longer the one sheepishly handing Simon over anymore. When I walked in that afternoon, she took him out of my hands and then smiled kindly in my direction. She had one of those perpetually warm faces, the kind that greets you like the sun even if you're mortal enemies.

"How's your mom?" she asked, tilting her head slightly so that her short blond hair shifted around her face. "I haven't seen her here in a while."

She searched my face for some news. She was on to me.

Crap.

"I'm so sorry to have to tell you this," I started, trying to find the right words people use when sharing terrible news with their dog groomer. "But my mom passed away."

She gasped audibly, her face crumbling. As she stared at me, silently, her eyes welled up, tears spilling down her face. I continued, not knowing what else to do. A wet poodle stared at me awkwardly from a grooming table behind her.

"She had cancer. Pancreatic cancer. It was really fast. She was only diagnosed, like, nine months ago."

The groomer was now quietly weeping. "Oh, my God," she said, "I am so sorry." She sucked in snot through her nose. Simon scowled. "I loved your mom," she said emphatically, nodding.

"Thank you," I muttered. "Yeah, she . . . uh. She really loved coming here to get Simon groomed."

Did she love coming here? She always said the groomer was nice, so it wasn't necessarily a lie. The groomer shifted a hand from underneath Simon's hunched frame and reached it across the counter, grabbing for mine. I kept going, the words vomiting out of my mouth. "I'm so sorry," I started, offering her up the same words I'd heard muttered at me a million times.

"It was peaceful," I said, pulling from the script I'd recited so many times that week. "We were all there with her—my brother and dad." Her hand was warm and firm, but it felt like holding a dead fish. I wanted to take her fingers and toss them across the room. "It was peaceful," I repeated again.

It hadn't been. It had been messy and terrible and my mom's limbs had turned dull and blue as the blood in her body worked overtime against her tumor.

This is the hard truth about delivering Dead Mom News. You lie to people. A lot. It's for their own good, of course; you don't want them to worry, or to even for a second imagine your mom zombied-out in a morphine coma, her sallow skin hanging off her cheekbones. You drop the "died peacefully" line so they can form their own version of how it went, imagining her propped up on pillows, sleeping soundly until her eyes fluttered one last time and she drifted off into Happy Death Land. They never know that the week before it happened you had to roll your mom—the woman who birthed you, held you, called on every birthday—on her side to try to shove an enema in her ass. You leave out how—just days before her death—you rubbed her back for hours, until your arms ached, in a futile, desperate attempt to alleviate her pain.

You tell everyone it was peaceful because you wish, so badly, that it had been. You lie because the lie is better than reality. You lie because you fear they can't handle the truth, and even worse—that you can't either. But lying over and over again is exhausting. I could barely bring myself to smooth it out anymore, to smile and nod when I really wanted to tell everyone, "It was horrible, and scary, and my mom became a ghost of herself, and I saw it all, and I am hurting."

But I tried one more time and comforted her, a lady whose name might have been Pam but could have also been Karen. I made a mental note to check the doggy report card later so I'd know what to call her next time, know whom to thank for her kind words. I gave her hand a quick squeeze and then yanked

it away, elbowing a rack of bejeweled dog collars. "Oops. Sorry."
I bent to pick up a black leather collar dotted with rhinestone
cupcakes. "Anyway," I said, shoving the collar back onto the
overstuffed rack. "Could you, um, also cut Simon's nails today?
They've gotten really long, and we're all too scared to do it."

She blinked at me, her lashes wet. I'd interrupted her in
the middle of her grieving. It was rude, cold, and my only way
out. "Thank you," I said, stepping back toward the door. "I'm
really sorry to have to tell you about my mom."

And with that I snuck out into the sharp March chill, collapsing in the driver's seat of my mom's car, her half-finished
water bottles frozen in the cup holders next to me.

I didn't want to do this anymore, this delivering of terrible
news. It was terrible news about *my own life*, and yet somehow having to be the one to break it to people meant having to
swallow my sorrow to make room for theirs. Thank God for the
Email List, the people who have to hear the news but aren't
quite close enough to warrant a phone call. These were Christmas card people—old family friends no one had spoken to for
years. I knew them solely through the notes they scribbled on
the inside of those cards. They existed once—our neighbors in
New Jersey who watched me when my brother was born, the
preschool friends who moved to Minneapolis. Now they were
just strangers I watched change on a yearly basis. I could not
tell you about the sound of their voice or what kind of music
they liked, but I knew their bad haircuts, when they got their
braces off, and who had made varsity soccer each year. They
were no more real to me than the characters I watched snip

at each other on TV each week, my own personal *Full House*. We were as foreign to them as they were to us, and most had no idea my mom had even been diagnosed with cancer. They probably wouldn't even be that broken up over my mom's death, I reasoned, and would respond with a quick email offering their condolences and be on their way.

This, I would come to discover, was an idiotic way to view other people's grief. I was way wrong—people who hadn't seen my mom in decades still cared deeply and were devastated by the news. But I hadn't truly understood their connection to my mom, or known much about the friendships they'd established when I was just a little kid. Plus, the gravity of my own sadness blocked me from considering anyone else's emotions. Pro tip: never underestimate the power of humans to still love and care for those they haven't seen in years.

After days spent calling people in tears over countless cups of tea gone cold, email felt like heaven. It was quick, clean, fast, and required the most minimal of emotional investments. Subject: Some Sad News. Copy and paste the script into the message, add a few flourishes to make it personal, and hit send. Easy.

I hammered out my emails and wandered into the kitchen, where I'd been eating my way through the many boxes of Kraft macaroni and cheese my mom had stockpiled over the years. She shopped as if the Big One was about to hit us anytime (we lived in Massachusetts, a state known for disasters like the 1986 World Series, not earthquakes), and we might just need to cover the house in Saran Wrap while eating an endless supply of baked beans. Just as the water started to bubble, the house phone rang. I let it go, choosing instead to dump the noodles in the pot before dragging the dog outside for a quick walk. Watching him sheepishly take a dump was way more enjoyable than human interaction. When we hustled back inside out of the cold, the light was blinking on our answering machine.

"Kate, this is That Random Blond Lady Who Was Friends with Your Mom Ten Years Ago but Then Moved to Seattle— You Know, The One with the Really Attractive Red-Haired Ivy-League-Educated Daughter Who Makes You Feel Inferior Every Time You Look at Our Christmas Card. I just received your email about your mom's death and want to speak to you immediately. I had no idea your mom was even sick. I'm in shock. I can't believe I am hearing this news over email. Please call me at [some number, probably 1-800-Hot-Smart-Daughter] as soon as possible."

I froze in the kitchen, as if she might be able to hear me moving through the answering machine and call me out for not picking up the phone. In my relief and excitement over the ease of emailing my bad news, I'd forgotten that there was someone on the other end receiving it. And the voice on the phone didn't sound empathetic or supportive. It sounded . . . *mad.* Like someone who felt robbed of details, annoyed that she hadn't been properly informed of exactly what was happening when it happened. She wasn't asking for a phone call back; she was demanding it. And so I did what any responsible adult would do. I emailed her back.

Hi there, I got your voice mail, I wrote, selecting my words carefully. I'd purposefully waited until late that night to send it, hoping that the time stamp would give the impression that I was incredibly busy dealing with important Dead Mom Stuff and therefore just could not find the time to pick up the phone.

I'm so sorry I can't talk. I'm just busy tying up loose ends here at my parents' house.

This was a lie. I was still at my parents' house, yes. But my loose ends consisted of wondering what to do with the half-finished quilt my mom left in pieces on our dining room table and figuring out where she kept the special lightbulbs needed for the downstairs bathroom. It was too dark to pee in there comfortably, and something had to be done. At night I watched hours of *Deal or No Deal*, polishing off a bottle of white wine as Howie Mandel droned on in the background. Most of the time I just sat on the couch, wondering how all this had happened. How, again, had my mom gotten sick and then died in just *nine months*? I could not wrap my head around it and was not in the mood to help anyone else comprehend it either.

I'm pretty busy and am not sure I will have time to call you back but please feel free to email me here and I'll do my best to get back to you. Thanks!

It had all the warmth of a work email, and I hoped she'd get the message.

She didn't. The phone rang again, this time at 10:45 at night. I recognized her number, the Pacific Northwest area code. I was well into my bottle of chardonnay, which I was planning on polishing off up in my bedroom, where I rolled empty bottles under my bed when they were done.* Upstairs

---

* I do not want to make light of drinking as a form of self-medication here. I definitely became a little too dependent on alcohol as a way to numb my pain during her illness and in the months after her death. I eventually formed healthier habits for dealing with my grief, but if you find yourself in the same boat, I recommend reaching out to a doctor or counselor for help.

my father was asleep, covered by my mom's blue felt bathrobe he'd been using as a blanket since she died. My dad hardly slept, so to put a stop to the ringing was reason enough to pick up the phone. But I didn't. Instead I stared at it as it rang, willing her to hang up with the power of my eyes.

The answering machine clicked on. It was my mother's voice. How had I not noticed that she was still on there?

"You have reached the Spencers," she said. "Please leave a message. Thank you."

It was that woman again, rattling on about how devastated she was by my mom's death and how she desperately needed someone—*anyone*—to call her back. But all I could hear was my mother, so calm and sweet on our answering machine. In that instant she felt so alive, even though I had seen her body laid out on a metal tray at the crematorium just days ago. Here was her voice talking to me through the answering machine, while her ashes sat upstairs in a wooden container the size of a shoebox, on top of the bedside table she'd been using just last week.

I had rattled off my script so many times, telling tons of people that she had died. And yet I had not processed my own words. She was everywhere, still: lingering on tabletops and dusty shelves, frozen in cup holders, echoing off the kitchen countertops. Sharing the news felt like a lie, because I didn't believe it myself.

My dad eventually called the woman back. She was shocked and sad, rightfully so. But I still had little patience for anyone else's grief. In hindsight, I wish I could have felt something for her, seen her suffering as more than just a nuisance. She had loved my mom, too, and known her in ways I had not. But I could barely look beyond myself and my own pain.

With each day that passed, I told more people the news, said the words in part just to convince myself. Over time they even started to roll off my tongue without me thinking about them, like when you finally become comfortable using the term "fiancé" after getting engaged. But there are moments, even now, when I tell someone that she's dead and the words still land with a plunk, naked and exposed. It catches me off guard, as if I'm hearing it for the first time. Oh right—*she's dead*. And maybe, telling other people is the *easy* part. The real challenge is simply breaking the news to yourself.

Hello there! If you're receiving this card it's because you've asked me about my dead mom. Thank you for your concern.

My mom died of _____. Yes, that is terrible.

Since you asked how I am doing the answer is (circle one):

- Great
- Terrible
- Somewhere in between
- Drunk

If there is anything you can do to help I will certainly let you know, but unless you can make my mom magically return to life I think I'm good for now.

Have a great day!

4

Death: The World's Most Awkward Hot Topic

Just when you think you've mastered the fine art of breaking the news about your dead mom, and told every person imaginable about it, a twist emerges, and suddenly your work is far from over. You see, now that you've transitioned into the "Everyone Knows" phase, you stumble upon people who want to talk about it. *A lot.* They exist in the most innocuous of places—at a party in line for the bathroom or standing in front of the dessert tray at a work luncheon. One minute you're innocently crossing your legs to hold in your pee, or loading four brownies onto a paper plate the size of a dime, and the next minute your arm is being stroked by someone you barely know, tenderly gazing into your eyes and asking, "So your mom died of [insert shitty mom-killer here]?"

I am not opposed to talking about my mom's death with people (Exhibit A: this book) and welcome a meaningful conversation about loss, grief, and how to ice your eyes after a good cry.* Finding strangers who can empathize with your loss can be comforting in the oddest of moments. But occasionally, there will be people who corner you for the Dead Mom Question Power Hour who may not have anything meaningful to add. Perhaps they're on a mission to understand their own mortality, or they're trying to empathize but don't quite know what to say. It's not that they mean you harm, but their desire to drag you into awkward conversations about your dead mom is, at the very least, annoying, and often comes at the weirdest of times. Watch out: these people almost always latch on at weddings, where endless white wine turns strangers into sensitive weepers who really want to give you a hug.

I met the WASP† at my dear friend Emma's bridal shower. It took place on one of those deliciously crisp New York City–spring days where the weather alone sends your good-mood hormones soaring. Still, I was just a couple months out from my mom's death, and no amount of gorgeous sunlight or blooming dogwood trees could completely distract me from my depression. This was a particularly precarious time in my social life, where I forced myself to return to my previously scheduled life activities, like after-work drinks and nodding along in loud bars as friends scream-shouted their very important opinions on *The Wire* at me over whatever Band of Horses song was wailing on the jukebox. In theory it felt good to go

---

* Frozen cucumber slices! Get on it.
† WASP stands for White Anglo-Saxon Protestant. If you ever come across a person who uses "summer" as a verb, they might be a WASP. (And this concludes my Jeff Foxworthy–esque stand-up routine.)

out and socialize, simply so I could check off a box on my
Seriously, I'm Fine! Look at Me Being a Functioning Member
of Society! list. But I was not myself. I moved through these
social interactions like a robot with artificial intelligence trying hard to appear human.

Lucky for me, I seemed to fool the WASP. A friend of the
groom's family, she was seated to my left at the long farm table
and was immediately my small-talk buddy. She had that shiny,
clean glow reserved solely for blond women from Connecticut,
like a wineglass on a store shelf before your fingerprints are
all over it. She was warm and a little too chatty, but I enjoyed
our conversations about kids and marriage, her shift from a
law career to stay-at-home-motherhood, and her recent small-
business venture. Who cares if I didn't know exactly how many
children she had or what her business actually was? She was
nice. And more importantly, she had no idea what had just
happened to my mother.

I had other close friends at the shower, seated nearby in
summery dresses and strappy sandals. But they were all pain-
fully familiar with the most miserable year of my life. The
WASP was a vacation from all the gory Dead Mom Details,
and I was enjoying her company like a daiquiri sipped with
an ocean view. Never once in our conversation over scrambled
eggs and mimosas did we touch on my mom, and I left relieved
that I'd met someone I could banter it up with at the wedding a few months later. We chatted over email a few times
in between, and she even went so far as to send me a gift—a
beautiful set of wineglasses—when she heard I got engaged.
I sent her a handwritten thank-you note in response, because

my mom was a stickler for good etiquette, and if she was going
to haunt me as a ghost it would almost certainly be because I
failed to write a thank-you note.

So I was genuinely excited when I finally found the WASP
at the wedding reception a few months later. We had so many
pressing topics to catch up on—the current weather (windy),
how stunning the bride looked (like a model), the delicious
crab cake appetizers (so adorably tiny and perfect for shoving in your mouth). We clinked wineglasses and hooked our
pashmina-covered arms together, our laughter carried across
the outdoor party by gusts of sea air. It was October in Maine,
the elements all signaling that winter was on its way to mess
everything up. We went though our usual small-talk routine,
and she caught me up on her job and kids. I nodded deliber-
ately as one does when sporting a bridesmaid updo, as if you're
balancing a newborn baby on your head.

"I didn't know you had *four* kids—and all boys!" I
exclaimed, chewing an ice cube. We were huddled together
like old friends, but I was still clueless about most of the
details of this woman's life. What town did she live in? What
was the WASP's middle name? Wait forget that—what was
her *last* name? I searched the walls of my brain, trying to recall
what I wrote on the envelope of that thank-you note months
ago but came up empty. But hey, no biggie—this is what weddings are all about. You become intense friends with fellow
guests for twenty-four to forty-eight hours, dance, laugh, and
take a questionable amount of tequila shots together. Maybe
there's some skinny-dipping at the hotel pool in the early
morning hours. The next morning you depart awkwardly and
later catch up solely through social media signals, liking each

other's photos on Facebook and Instagram, but never actually speaking again. Besides, the WASP was still my safe space. My mom had only been dead six months now, and I wanted nothing more than to avoid the topic completely. To my friends and fiancé, I was still the girl grieving her dead mom. But the WASP didn't know this side of me, and that alone made her my favorite person in the world.

"Let me introduce you to some people," she said as we grabbed some chicken skewers off a server's tray. She led me over to a group of women, all uniformed in pearls and salt-and-pepper bobs. They opened the circle, welcoming us. Just as I was about to charm them with my wine-induced humor and wit, the WASP piped up.

"Everyone, this is the bride's friend Kate," she said, drawing out the words. "Her mom just died of *cancer*."

My stomach ate itself as she spoke. *What did she just say?*

"Oh dear," clucked one of the Gray Ladies. "What kind?"

"Um, pancreatic," I replied, gulping down the rest of my wine.

"That must be so hard," the WASP said, her eyes big and wet. The group nodded. "We're all so glad you are strong enough to be here."

Sure, it was no secret that my mom had recently died, and I didn't mind people sharing the information or knowing about it. After all, "Her mom just died" is often a thing whispered about you behind your back from a place of kindness, to excuse you for your social awkwardness or seemingly random bursts of crying.

But she had never once mentioned to me that she was up on my Dead Mom History. What, I wondered, could inspire the WASP to use this as her opening line when introducing me? Did she pity me? Was she proud? Showing me off? Trying to matchmake me with other Dead Moms Club members? I have so many other great qualities; I can burp the alphabet and had recently paid off my credit card debt and then spent my savings on a new Marc Jacobs bag. Surely she could have opened with something else so I didn't have to spend my friend's wedding fielding sympathetic looks from aunts in crystal-covered reading glasses with stale vodka breath.

I nodded along, trying to play it cool. But my face had that look of horror that busts out when you accidentally come across crime scene photos on Google Image. Here I was, trying to avoid Dead Mom Talk by attaching myself to someone I thought would never bring it up. Now I was shoulder-to-shoulder with a group of women who were using my Dead Mom Story as a launching pad for their own Cancer Is the Worst stories. And it is! The worst! But it's not the thing I want to talk about as a warm-up to shimmying in a circle to "I Wanna Dance with Somebody." Dead Mom Talk does not get me in the mood to dance slightly too close to someone's sweaty uncle. Having a team meeting about cancer was the last thing I wanted to be doing at my friend's wedding.

I broke free from the WASP and latched onto my group of girlfriends, avoiding her tender stares for the rest of the night. And from that second on, I swore off wedding friendships. Never again, no sir. I was now strictly a Hang Out with Only People You Know Very Well type of wedding guest. I was done with older women with enviably huge but still somehow understated diamond earrings and a proclivity toward awkward Dead Mom Talk.

Until it happened again a few months later.

This time I was near the beach, sunburnt and sweating in a way that would have made my pasty English and Scottish ancestors proud. It was a gorgeous wedding, the beauty of the day outshone only by the bride and groom, who were radiant and stunning in all their newlywed glory. Later that night, as the seafood buffet began to shut down, a giant dance party exploded. A circle grew, men in loafers without socks and women in bright Lily Pulitzer dresses shaking it to Lionel Richie. My squad eagerly joined in, chugging rum and cokes and clumsily sashaying around on stomachs full of crab legs. I lifted my hands to signal to the world that I just don't care, when suddenly, an older woman with a sleek, dark bob grabbed me by the arm. We had been introduced once before because she lived in my hometown. She had the polished look of someone with a closet full of tennis skirts at home.

"Woohoo!" I sang-screamed, because I had zero idea what her name was. I turned toward her, revealing two-foot-long pit stains, thinking she was about to twirl me around. Instead she pulled me close and shouted in my face. Was she about to kiss me?

"Was your mom the one who was hit by the car?"

"What?" I screamed back, shaking my hips. Surely she didn't just ask—

"WAS YOUR MOM THE ONE WHO WAS HIT BY THE CAR?" she yelled again, her spit hitting my cheeks. This time she was loud enough for me to understand every word.

My brain pushed the booze aside long enough to put together what was happening. I blinked and swayed on my platform espadrilles as I pieced it together. She had confused my mom with another woman from our town with kids my age, who had been out on a walk and was struck by a car. It was an awful and tragic story, but it was not mine.

"No," I shouted. "My mom died of pancreatic cancer."

We were still dancing. We looked like extras at a school dance on *Saved by the Bell*, two strangers gyrating with a bit too much excitement because we didn't actually know how to move.

She nodded and swayed our arms, still attached. "Well," she shouted again. "You're very pretty."

She offered a flat smile and then released her hand, boogying away like a one-woman conga line. I kept moving, as if shaking my ass and waving my arms would somehow erase the entire interaction. But I couldn't squeeze the conversation out of my brain. It felt like a violation of the universal code of conduct for weddings. Rule number one: don't hit on the bride or groom. Rule number two: drink water in between cocktails so you don't become That Guest. Rule number three: don't randomly walk up to other guests and incorrectly guess how their moms died.

All I wanted was to pose for selfies with my friends in peace and pound as many different fruit tarts off the dessert table as I could fit into my stomach. (I also want a second season of *Freaks and Geeks*, if you're keeping a list.) I was not interested in being the go-to person for awkward conversations about my saddest thing.

But once I got past how annoying these conversations were for me, I could see something that connected both the WASP and the Wedding Shouter, something beyond their toned middle-aged lady arms and shampoo-commercial hair: They

were trying. In their own awkward, uncomfortable, slightly
socially inappropriate ways, they were attempting to connect.
To sympathize. To show kindness and care.

These are easy things to expect from others. But boy, are
they hard to deliver. And sure, they both kinda failed at it. But
I appreciate that at the core of their weirdness was good inten-
tion. It's awkward, but it's something. Because I'm sure that they
tried to say the right thing, even if it did come out totally wrong.

I t's not that anyone intentionally *tries* to have awkward conversations about death. We've all done it, because it's a hard
topic to be cool about. Death has no chill. But sometimes a
miracle occurs when you're stuck in one of these uncomfortable back-and-forths: you find someone who gets it.

Three weeks after my mom died, and a few months before
I met the WASP, I took the bus from Boston to New York City
to see Anthony, perform at my regular improv comedy show
(I'm hilarious in the wake of personal tragedy, lemme tell you),
and venture out to a friend's loft party.* It was crowded and
smelled like ripe, onion-y body odor, and it was the exact distraction I needed after nine months of nonstop cancer. Lots

---

* Now would be a good time to mention that anyone who judges how
  you grieve and scolds you for how you should be grieving can go take
  a long walk on a long pier and think about how stupid they are. If you
  want to hide inside for a week (or longer!), awesome. But if you want
  to go out to parties, that's fine, too. There will always be someone
  who thinks you should be holed up, weeping, for the rest of your life.
  Feel free to remind those people that your mom is *dead* and mourning forever isn't going to bring her back. Neither is dancing wildly in
  a sea of hot, sweaty bodies, but at least it's a little more fun.

of friends there knew about my mom's recent death, but there were plenty of people who had no idea who I was other than the tall girl with a slight muffin top double-fisting keg cups. It was heaven.

At some point deep in the night I landed in the quiet corner of the party, in line for beer. The petite, black-haired woman in front of me caught my eye, looked down at the necklace dangling against my Old Navy tank top, and refocused her gaze like a laser.

"Is that a locket?" she asked, beer on her breath.

"Yup," I replied, my voice short.

"Do you have photos inside of it?" she responded immediately. I nodded. I knew where this was going.

"Who are they of?" She wasn't asking anymore; she was demanding, so intent on digging info out of me she hadn't noticed it was her turn to refill her beer.

"My mom and grandmother," I answered, using my most I Don't Want to Talk About It tone. I stacked my cups and reached up with my free hand to touch the locket, just to make sure it was still there. It was one of those things that was so special to me it was stupid to wear it out, but I was also terrified to leave it at home, certain a burglar would drop by and determine it was the one thing he had to have.

The locket had been my mother's, but for only the last month of her life. That February she'd landed in the hospital again, needing yet another procedure to keep her growing tumor from shutting down her stomach completely. She was sick and weak, and on top of it all she was mourning the loss of her own mom, who had died just weeks earlier. That's right, my dying mom was a brand-new member of the Dead Moms

Club. This was the shit-show nightmare we were living in: endless death and sadness. She spent the entire hospital stay in tears.

At one point, her nurse, a big, gruff woman with all the warmth of New England in winter, noticed her crying and bent down next to her on the hospital bed.

"What's wrong?" she asked, her Boston accent adding extra syllables to every word. She sounded irritated by the distraction.

"My mother just died," she said, defensively. "She was ninety, and it was her time, but . . . " she trailed off, sniffling. "I still miss her."

"Oh, honey." The nurse's body shifted as she sat down on the bed, her body weight lifting my mom like a crane.

"My own mom died this year, and you know what I did?" She reached for a chain around her neck and popped open the locket at the end so my mom could have a look.

"I keep her here. That way she's still with me, even though she's not."

After she'd left, my mom summoned me over. "I want a locket with a picture of Gramy in it," she said urgently. I nodded and booked it out of the hospital, eager for a chore that didn't involve a trip to the medical supply store. (You can only buy so many incontinence bed pads before you descend into a very dark place.) I found a small silver locket at a mall kiosk and had the dude at the photo store shrink a picture of my grandmother's head and pop it in the locket. By the time Mom was back home, the locket was around her neck. It stayed there until the night she died, when I lifted her head, undid the clasp, and put it around my own neck.

I added a photo of her in there, of course. It was one of the first things I did after she died, and I'd worn it every day since. Still, it was the first time someone had noticed and asked about it, and worse—not backed down. My mom had died just nineteen days earlier (yes, I was counting), and her death had yet to become my reality. I was still grabbing for my phone five times a day to call her.

The girl was staring at me, oblivious to my signals. "So," she said, slurring as one does in a keg line at one AM. "They're dead, right?"

"Um, it's your turn to use the keg," I replied, pointing to her position at the front of the line.

"My mom is dead," she said, somehow holding eye contact while bending over the giant silver barrel. "She sends me signs. Just last week I woke up to a raven staring at me through my bedroom window, and when I got home he was still there, waiting."

"Did your mom love birds or something?" I asked, relaxing. This was the first time since my mom's death that I'd talked to someone else my age with a dead parent.* It was more comforting than I expected, as if I were suddenly with my people, even though my people consisted of one very drunk girl with red lipstick on her teeth.

"No," she said. "But I'm from Baltimore. She was *obsessed* with the Ravens. Of course she'd come back as their mascot."

She was nosy, drunk, and a stranger; I had no idea what her name was, and—oh wait, what's that? She has a dead mom, too? Well, *hello* there.

---

* Other than Anthony, who joined the Dead Moms Club in 2002.

The second she fessed up, I was on board. Suddenly this wobbly, hammered girl got me in a way most of my friends did not. My irritation shifted to adoration in seconds; I got why she was so relentless in her questioning. She was looking for an ally, trying to ascertain if I was like *her*. Now I wanted nothing more than to drag her off to a corner and ask: *How the hell am I going to get through this?*

"I'm pretty sure my mom attended her funeral reception as a bug," I said, my voice low. "She loved insects, and that day there was a weird beetle in our living room. And it's March— why would there be beetles out in March?" I paused, feeling relieved to get this off my chest. "I haven't even told my boy-friend that."

She leaned in and gave my arm a squeeze.

"Here," she said, handing me the beer she'd poured. "I don't even want this. I just stayed in line because I thought you might also be a Dead Mom person."

"Thanks." I smiled. "I guess I am."

Breaking news: we're all going to die. Yet illness, death, and grief occupy such a small space of our cultural conversation. Why are we all so awkward when it comes to one of the biggest things every single one of us is going to get to do in life?

Anyone who's had the topic of their dead mom forced on them can attest: it can ruin your whole night and send you for a ride on your own personal crazy train. One second you're minding your own business, and then suddenly you're a pawn in someone else's Learning How to Process Grief game. But there's a fine line to walk here, between protecting yourself from soul-sucking conversations and possibly blocking yourself off from a connection that might actually *help* you. And so I say this: be wary, but be open. Be kind, but don't put someone else's needs before your own. Listen, but don't lose your own voice. And most importantly, learn how to politely leave a conversation. Or just do what I do: say you have to pee, and then never come back to the party. Works every time.

EIGHT SASSY DEAD MOM COMEBACKS IN HANDY LISTICLE FORM

(Because if you need someone to feed you lines, Cyrano de Bergerac style, I'm your girl.)

- I'd like to talk about something else, please.
- We tell people she died of [insert real reason here], but actually she joined the CIA and was then recruited to spy for North Korea, and the government is covering it all up and making us lie about it. *Whisper* *But you seem like someone I can trust.*
- What's a mother?
- No, she's alive—she's just been focused on becoming the world's oldest Snapchat star.
- Yeah, yeah, sure, my mom died, but can you believe the Bachelor is still living forever on TV?
- Actually, my mom is Oprah Winfrey, and this conversation is not one of her favorite things.

- You're right, she *is* in a better place now. She just texted me from Waffle House. Which is really crazy because she's dead.
- Let's talk about your dead mom instead. Oh, she's still alive? Wow, aren't you lucky?

5

The Weight of It All

There was an upside to the endless conversations I had with other people about death: I could avoid the awful, hurt-so-bad-my-body-literally-ached-all-the-time pain I was in. Talking to people gave me an out. When you chat with them about grief—even if it's your own—it's not entirely about you. And you can deflect—talk about them, share the focus, listen to their own painful stories. But when you're alone with your sadness, you're faced with a choice:

1. Really tackle it, despite that being an excruciatingly painful, exhausting, and terrifying process, OR . . .
2. Avoid the hell out of it!

We all know which one I chose, right? No one actually thinks I was pragmatic and actually addressed my issues, do you? Nope. Instead of facing my grief, I joined Weight Watchers just a month after my mom died. It was a great plan! I was already often too depressed to eat. So why not capitalize on this exciting opportunity and lose ten pounds?!

Answer: Because I was in an extremely dysfunctional and turbulent time in my life. My chaos transferred right over to the Weight Watchers program immediately, where I lost twenty-five pounds and found myself face-to-face with some seriously disordered eating.*

Now let me preface this by saying that Weight Watchers did not *give* me an eating disorder. (I don't want to get sued, and also I love Oprah Winfrey's Weight Watchers commercials way too much to ever disparage the brand.) But what it did give me were the things I so desperately craved during that awful time of my life: order, control, support, and two-point chocolate-covered brownies. Instead of dealing with my sadness spiral, I began obsessively restricting my diet, exercising, and attending the weekly meetings with a fervor.

If you've never done Weight Watchers—hi, who are you?— allow me to explain how it works. The system has changed a bit since I first used it, but it goes something like this: Food and drinks are assigned a point value, and you're given a target amount of points to consume each day, as well as some bonus points for when you want to eat an ice cream sundae or drink a bottle of tequila or—better yet—both. Exercise is also tracked as points. Soon you start to see the world in points only. You move through the world like some sort of Weight Watchers Terminator—you can scan a grocery store aisle and the point values of food will pop up in front of your eyes.

---

* Disclaimer: No doctor ever diagnosed me with an eating disorder, but the whole experience involved eating (or not) and certainly seemed very disordered.

At the start of each meeting you are weighed in privately by an eager fifty-something woman with a nickname like Barb who enjoys *Downton Abbey* and chunky costume jewelry. You take off your shoes, put a paper towel down on the scale because feet germs are a real thing, and watch as your weight appears on a digital screen on Barb's desk. She then hands you a sticker that lists both your current weight and your total weight lost, which you stick into a little white booklet. Then you slap a giant name tag on your chest and saddle up for the meeting: thirty to forty-five minutes of eating tips, conversation, and head nodding in solidarity.

When I joined, I was 160-ish pounds. My height is somewhere around "Did you play basketball in high school?"* feet tall. I was not overweight by any standard; according to Weight Watchers I was within the healthy weight range for my height. (And I still am. I win!) I definitely didn't *need* to lose weight; no doctor had suggested it, and my health was good. But I had always struggled with body dysmorphia and feeling "big," which happens when you reach your adult height of five foot ten—boobs 'n' all—in the fifth grade. Plus, I was unemployed, in desperate need of a distraction, and so depressed I could barely walk straight. I needed an activity, something to get me out of the house and around other people. And most importantly, I had once read an interview with Tina Fey in which she outed herself as a Weight Watchers member, and as Tina Fey goes, so goes Kate Spencer. I was on board.

I signed up in April, exactly one month after my mom had died, set my goal weight at 150 pounds, and started tracking my

* I did not.

points. It was surprisingly easy—I just counted and tracked, counted and tracked. But at the same time, I started obsessively exercising, too. Moving my body was the only way I was able to shed some of the grief that had hijacked my bones and skin and seeped into my muscle. I couldn't yet find the words to describe the pain I was in, but every time a yoga teacher pushed my body into a heart-opening pose, it felt as if my grief was cracking open, like an eggshell hitting the side of a frying pan. I would sob and shake in class, attempting to hold it all in until we got to the savasana portion of class, right at the end. The second I flattened my body against the mat I'd cry fat tears into the lavender-scented eye pillow the teacher had pressed against my face. When the lights came back on, I used that same pillow like a tissue to dry up my tears, as if nothing had happened.

Here is a dirty secret about Weight Watchers: there are tricks to weighing in, sneaky moves people make to weigh as little as possible. Conveniently, my yoga studio was located directly across the hall from the Weight Watchers office, so I'd hit up yoga class right before a meeting, making sure to weigh in wearing my tiny yoga shorts and a tank top, the least amount of clothes possible. You strip down to the lightest clothes you have—tank tops and shorts—and you never get on the scale with shoes on. Oftentimes people avoid drinking a lot of water before a weigh-in, since it can add weight to your body. And you always pee before a weigh-in, just to get that extra water weight out. Even taking off jewelry can help shed .001 of a pound. You develop rituals, superstitions about your weigh-in that you convince yourself hold the secret to your weight loss. For me it was that I always had to weigh in after yoga, when my body was sweaty, empty of water, and growling for dinner. Perfect.

At first I hid in the back of the meetings, certain I'd never participate or gain anything from going. But as weeks went by, I inched my way up to the front row. We announced our weight loss achievements—2.4 pounds, 0.6 pounds—and clapped for each other, the group leader rewarding us with stickers as if we were kindergarteners. I displayed them on my booklet, which I hid in my wallet.

These meetings became my safe space, my panic room away from the chaos of my grief and emotions. Tracking my food centered and calmed me, like some sort of meditation practice. I started every day with a packet of instant oatmeal, ate rice cakes for snacks, lunched on a salad or vegetarian sushi. Each night I ate the same thing: steamed kale with lemon and olive oil, a homemade Greek salad, and one sugar-free container of Jell-O. I craved the structure of this menu, so much so that anytime I had to eat out, my heart would race with panic.

Meanwhile, my body gave in and started doing something it had never done before: it obeyed. The weight slid off my body. I hit 150 pounds in May and decided to keep going, checking off 145 come June. I bought myself new clothes at Banana Republic to celebrate. (I really know how to go wild, let me tell you.) That month I attended a friend's baby shower at a quaint Brooklyn cafe. Beforehand, I proudly examined the menu online so I'd know exactly what to order, and I felt such a sense of accomplishment when I asked the waitress to bring me my Eggs Florentine without the hollandaise sauce. Nothing felt better to me than being in control of my food intake. It was such a relief to have the power to deny or grant myself permission to eat. To decide to lose weight and then do it gave me the greatest sense of calm I'd ever experienced. I was healthy, happy, free, and fit!

Except, of course, I wasn't. My new restrictive behavior did nothing to actually curb the turmoil I was in. And I developed a strange habit, where I'd breathe air into my stomach—like when you're trying to force your body to burp—and then let the air out slowly, a quiet, whispered rumble. I'd do it when I was hungry, to trick my body into thinking it was full, or when I was stressed trying to meet a deadline at work. Eventually it blew up into a full-on habit, and I was quietly burping at all hours of the day. At home Anthony would beg me to stop because the sound of me burping constantly grossed him out so much. This is a very normal reaction to have when the person you've committed to make out with for life can't stop belching. But I'd lost all control over it, and soon it became second nature, like biting my nails.

The Weird Burping Thing (this is its medical name) satisfied two itches: my desire to control my eating, and my raging anxiety. And as I kept losing weight, the hunger to see the scale go farther and farther down intensified. My goal weight had been 150, but then I tempted myself by adjusting it to 145, and then 142.

"I just want to see if I can do it!" I told the lady at the desk as I stood on the scale. She adjusted my goal with an excited fervor. "Good luck!" One forty-two came easily, so then I scratched that and went for 140. "Congrats!" the weigh-in lady said, handing over my weight card. I was 139 pounds. But I couldn't stop now; I was drunk on weight loss. I had to see how low I could go. And so I asked the woman to reset my goal weight again. "I'd like to try for 138," I told her. This time, I was met with a furrowed brow. "How tall are you?" she asked, tilting her eyes up at me. I had obsessively reviewed the Weight Watchers weight guidelines in anticipation of this question. For a five-foot-ten woman, the advisable weight range was 139–169. Weight Watchers wouldn't let you make your goal weight lower than your prescribed range; it was against the Weight Watchers law. So I did the logical thing. I lied.

"I'm, like, five eight," I told her with a convincing nod. "Maybe five nine." Satisfied, she tapped a few keys and handed me my weight book. I hit 136 a couple weeks later. My lowest weight was 135.6. Everyone clapped when I announced it in the meeting.

It is hard to explain the hold the weight loss had over me. I'm not sure I totally understand it even now. Something about it still intoxicates me, even though I can see how disordered it all was. It wasn't simply nice to control my life. It was, sadly, also just nice to be super thin. I received more attention than I ever had about my looks: compliments, approving looks, saleswomen oohing and awing over my body when I easily slid into size 27 J Brand jeans. Wedding dress shopping was a pile-on of compliments because I could fit into the sample sizes, and I was grabbing size zero dresses off the racks at Anthropologie and zipping into them easily. Zero! I couldn't believe my good luck. At the time, I imagined everyone so mesmerized by how skinny I was that they surely had no idea I was actually a hot mess of raw sadness. In hindsight, I now know that my friends who offered comments like, "Hey, I can see all the vertebrae in your back" with concern in their eyes were on to me.

I rode the Weight Watchers train right up to my wedding but gave up tracking my points during our honeymoon in Hawaii. The days were filled with pure happiness: eating, drinking, celebrating, sunburning. But at night, I'd gaze in the mirror and pinch my stomach, convinced that I was rapidly gaining the weight back. When we landed in New York, I raced back to Weight Watchers and weighed in at around 140 pounds. I panicked and set off to get my weight back down to my cherished 136. I spent a week restricting my food intake to just fruit, vegetables, and brown rice, and knocked a couple of pounds back off. But I could never get back into the swing of it all. Tracking my food felt less like a relief and more like a chore. I flaked on meetings, choosing instead to hang out with my husband or meet my friends for margaritas and nachos downtown. I was frustrated with myself—why was my ability to restrict my diet slowly dwindling?

It took therapy to help me figure it out. (Turns out, it would take therapy to help me figure *a lot* of things out.) At my first session a few months after our wedding, I wedged myself in the corner of my therapist's musty, stained gray couch. I made a mental note of where the closest box of tissues was in the room: coffee table, check. And then, after attempting small talk and a chipper recap of my family life, I finally revealed the thing that terrified me so much it felt almost impossible to say: "I'm still, like, just processing the fact that my mom even *got* cancer," I blubbered, my snot too powerful for the generic tissues I yanked out of the box on the coffee table. "I'm not even dealing with the fact that she died yet."

You know what they say: before you can heal, you gotta deal. (No one says this. I just made it up. I'm sorry.) Every week I showed up, I sat on the smelly couch, and I cried the anger out. Grief loosened its grip on my life, just a little bit. Eventually, I stopped needing Weight Watchers to help me survive each day. The urge to control my life lessened. I remembered how good it felt to eat without concern-trolling myself over each bite.

But eventually I had to do something terrible. I had to actually deal with the emotions that stewed inside me over my mom's death. And there was one awful, ugly one that scared me in particular:

I was mad. I *am* mad.

I am very, very angry that I do not have a mom.

It's been ten years, and so I can navigate my anger with some ability, kind of like how I can mostly use chopsticks but sometimes still need a spoon to pick up leftover bits of rice. But just knowing how to manage your anger doesn't make it go away. And I'm pretty sure it's never going to go away, ever.

So let me just get it all out right here: I am furious that she is gone. All those icky, uncomfortable emotions we loathe to admit we have—rage, resentment, jealousy, and good old-fashioned hatred—have bubbled up and out of me at various times as I've grieved. Navigating the motherless world is hard enough (who is supposed to tell me if this shirt looks bad?), but the emotional strife is an added bonus no one warns you about

when you begin your journey down the garbage chute that
is grieving. Sometimes the depths of your sadness and anger
will shock you; there will be times when you will hate people
with a murderous rage, simply because they still have their
moms and you do not. You will hate strangers sitting across
from you on the bus yelling into their iPhones at their moms
on the other end. You will hate your friends who complain
about all the annoying things their moms do, the things you'd
give anything to still experience and get pissed off about. You
will hate the moms you see walking hand in hand with their
adult children or slowly pushing grandkids down the street in
strollers. You will hate people who have terrible living moms,
even though you know that's unfair and understand that some
moms can be horrible, garbage humans, too. You will hate and
hate and hate, and it will terrify you.

When I was first able to pinpoint this weird, surging thing
inside me as anger, I was surprised. The feeling embarrassed
me, so much so that I bounced straight from my anger right
over to feeling deeply ashamed of it. I found it hard to tell anyone about it, even my almond-faced therapist with her silky
blond hair and kind, understanding eyes. My anger felt different from the kind I was "supposed" to have. It wasn't a raging
fury that my mother was dead, exactly. It was more that I was
mad at everyone else around me. We all were living boring,
predictable lives.* The only difference was most people got to
go home and tell their living, breathing, sensible-jean-wearing
moms all about it.

---

* Rihanna excluded.

And I was mad at people simply because they had moms. Oh, how I *hated* them for it.* I was too scared and mortified to tell anyone, so when friends asked how I was doing, I nodded and gave them my rehearsed "Some days are hard, but I'm okay" answer.

My anger was conceived, nurtured, and birthed during the one second I found out my mother was sick. Sure, I had all the other standard emotions that come with a Dying Mom: denial, depression, sadness, the ability to eat box after box of Wheat Thins despite having had dinner just thirty minutes before. But the anger was there from the start, and it bubbled over constantly. I hated everyone who crossed my path, from the overly concerned social worker at the hospital to the nutritionist who gave my mom a milk-shake recipe, complimented our matching mother-daughter pants, and then sent us on our way. After she died, my rage strangled everything around me like a throbbing hate-tentacle.

It's a cliché to claim there are no words to describe the emotional acid trip that is grief. But anyone who's been through it knows that words just don't do it justice. Grief poisons every corner of your life, fogging up your brain with sadness so deep that just breathing can hurt. Even after my mom died, and I went back to living full-time with Anthony, found a fun, new job, went out with friends for sushi, jogged slowly along the Hudson River, it felt as if I were doing all these things while stoned. I was high on my sorrow and never quite fully present.

---

* If you're a friend reading this and wondering, "Wait, did she hate me?" the answer is yes. I'm sorry. It's not personal. And I don't really hate you. I love you. Like, a lot.

It was a thick, hazy goo that covered every part of my life, like a cobweb that sticks to you no matter what you do to shake it loose. Grief is a sort of weird superpower: it paralyzes you, but you're able to keep moving forward while simultaneously being eaten alive by your pain. It is also a cockroach: it can live through any apocalypse you throw its way.

I was so wounded by my mother's death, and the fury I felt, that I could barely speak about it. Sure, I was able to give a clinical rundown of what had happened. It's a story you get used to telling, and one that you can recite without actually thinking about the words you're saying. "Yeah, my mom died of pancreatic cancer. She was stage four when she was diagnosed, so she only lived for nine months. It spread to her liver. It was hard, but my family did hospice, and it was really meaningful that we all got to be together." But inside I would churn with rage, fury, and dark coils of sadness. These emotions felt endless inside me. I'd show up at therapy and spit them up on the floor. But they just kept coming, like a magician doing that creepy trick where he pulls an endless rope of scarves out of his mouth.

These feelings don't just go away. They linger. Hover. They are with me always. Even at my most functioning—when I am a patient mother, and a productive employee, and can afford to regularly highlight my hair—they are there, watching me. These emotions are my roommates now, bunking up beside me at night. They do not pay any rent; they eat all my Pirate's Booty; they delete my recordings of *Bachelor in Paradise* off my DVR. They are determined to ruin me, and yet I can never fully evict them from my brain.

I have tried—really tried—to chip away at my grief, to name it, package it, place it in its proper spot on my emotional shelf. But lately I've just given up. I'm finally giving it permission to breathe and exist. It's never been a neat, concise package, like the Kübler-Ross Five Stages of Grief suggest. Denial, anger, bargaining, depression, acceptance—they didn't show up in that order, with a gentle knock at the door. Sometimes one appears; other times they barge in together, a surly mob. And then there are their cousins: shock, horror, relief, confusion, despair, and the black sheep of the family, happiness.

Most days now, they lie dormant in me. Sometimes it gets so quiet in my brain I think they've finally packed up and left. But every year, as the calendar rounds the corner to March and the anniversary of her death approaches, anger bubbles again. I snap at my kids more; I rage over the smallest of things, screaming behind the steering wheel of my car when another driver forgets to use their blinker. At first I'm perplexed, and then I remember: it's here again. And I am still mad. So mad. I can starve it, avoid it, rationalize it, manage it, talk about it in therapy, and eat it up in neat little points value. No matter how much weight I lose, I will never lose this one simple truth: I want my mom. I so am fucking mad that she's gone. And that feeling will never, ever die.

GRIEF: A MENU

AMUSE-BOUCHE
Your Earliest Childhood Memory

APPETIZER
The Smell of Her Shirt When She Hugged You Close
as a Kid

FIRST COURSE
Hazy Visions of Her Smiling at You as You Walked
into School on the First Day of Kindergarten

SECOND COURSE
Memories of Her Driving You to Soccer Practice for
Years, with a Sprinkle of Regret for Never Appreciat-
ing It

THIRD COURSE
A Smorgasbord of Fights, from Childhood to That
Awful One Just a Few Weeks Before She Died

DESSERT
A Delicious Scoop of Remembering How She Always
Cried When She Felt Proud of You

Bon appétit!

6

Family

"They won't talk to me." My mom stood in our kitchen, our old white plastic phone in her hand.

"Who?" I asked from the kitchen counter, where I was indulging in my time-honored tradition of dipping pretzels into a tub of Kraft Philadelphia whipped cream cheese and shoving them into my mouth.

"Your grandparents," she sighed. My dad's parents. "Ever since I got sick, they refuse to even ask me how I'm doing. When I answer the phone, they just ask to talk to Dad, and then ask *him* about it."

Moments earlier she had shouted upstairs to my dad to pick up the phone. Now I watched her press the receiver back to her ear, eavesdropping on his conversation with his mom and dad. She eventually hung up and wandered away, uncharacteristically crestfallen.

My parents were married when they were twenty and twenty-one, two baby-faced, shaggy-haired, broke college students who were gifted twenty joints from a friend as a wedding present (1972 was everything we imagined it to be, apparently!).

The idea of a wedding had not been particularly popular with either set of parents, and they tag-teamed as a unit to convince my overeager, in-love parents to postpone their wedding a year, to make sure they were really down for the whole "'til death do us part" thing. They were.

My dad's mom being Italian American meant that my grandfather was Italian American, too, by default, even though he was of German and English heritage. If an Italian claims you, you better adopt their heritage or run. Everything in my dad's family—besides his last name—was heavily Italian: the food we ate at Thanksgiving, the Roman Catholic church my grandma attended, the relatives who crammed onto their couches every night. My grandmother, Elsie, loved my husband, Anthony, simply because he has an Italian name. It didn't matter that he wasn't Italian at all (literally, not a drop), just the suggestion of some sort of connection to Italy, mixed with his jet-black hair, earned him points. Needless to say, my Protestant mother who grew up in the woods of New Hampshire was a bit of a conundrum. But Italian Americans are as kind and welcoming as they are critical and opinionated. Once you get on their good side, you're family for life. It didn't take my mom much time to win over my gregarious, pint-sized grandmother and my hardened (but surprisingly weepy and tender, especially in his old age) grandfather.

My mom had that thing that's so often rare to come by: pure warmth and grace. She was one of those unassumingly kind and easy people whose demeanor welcomes you in, like a bowl of soup on a blustery day. And she had done something incredibly important in my grandmother's eyes: she'd made my dad, her "Jimsy," happy.

My grandparents had never been particularly strong com-
municators, though, especially when it came to the hard stuff
like, oh, *death*. Terrified of burdening people with their emotions, they simply didn't share them. And you couldn't really
blame them: they were both the children of immigrants,
working-class kids trying to get by. For them the Depression was
a lived experience, not a topic for history class or a punch line
on *Seinfeld*. My grandfather's tough exterior formed as a kid,
when he had to get a job at eleven years old after his father died.
My grandmother worked hard to fit in with American culture,
changing her incredibly Italian last name from Delli Franci to
Del France to assimilate. When my grandfather returned from
World War II, they got married, walking down the aisle on a
Monday morning because the church would be full of fresh
flowers left over from Sunday's funerals, saving them a good
chunk of dough. Even though they came to enjoy a reasonably
stable, middle-class life, my grandmother still had a tendency
to snatch whatever "free" things she came across: sugar packets
from restaurants and silverware and salt and pepper shakers
from airline meals.* They had lived through extraordinarily difficult times, where sucking things up in silence and persevering
was just something you did. Meanwhile, I struggle with a debil-
itating addiction to Twitter and can't stop posting on Facebook
about it. I have their hard work and perseverance to thank for
the privilege of being able to live my life as a self-absorbed dolt.

My grandmother only mentioned my mother to me once
after she died. We were out to lunch, a visit over seafood at
a coastal Connecticut restaurant. "It was awful," she said

---

* Note to my younger readers: airlines once served real food on trays,
like tiny cafeterias rocketing through the sky!

quietly, "what happened to Martha." Caught off guard, I couldn't find a response fast enough. By the time my mouth formed the word "yeah," she had already moved on to talking about how warm the dinner rolls were.

I knew my whole life that my dad's family didn't talk about death. It happened, respects were paid, and then the silence kicked in. And that started long before my mother.

Growing up, my dad lived directly across the street from his cousin Johnny. They were close in age, so naturally they were allies, spending their days together riding their bikes around their neighborhood or running back and forth between their houses. When my dad was ten, Johnny, eleven, died tragically, in an awful accident that sounds like something out of *My Girl* 3, a movie that doesn't exist but should. The charcoal grill Johnny's dad was using exploded after the lighter fluid ignited, and Johnny ended up with burns covering most of his body. He died a few months later. Despite their friendship, my dad wasn't allowed to attend the funeral, and his death was rarely spoken about in the family again. Not because they didn't care, but because it wasn't done.

My aunt Leslie also died of cancer, back in the mid-'90s. She married my dad's middle brother when I was seven and immediately assumed the role of Glamorous Aunt, tall and beautiful and always with a full face of makeup highlighting her olive skin. She had the vibe of a blurry, pastel painting of a beach at sunset. I worshipped all my aunts, but there was just something about Leslie—her silky, puffy '80s blouses, her hair teased and sprayed just right, her shoulders padded like a couch—that left my eyes wide. Women in my WASPy town didn't dress in bright colors; my mom favored wearing black to weddings, and the only makeup I ever saw her use was a red Cover Girl eyeliner pencil that somehow made her look more severe. My mom was beautiful and elegant, but in that "my Puritan ancestors slept on cold beds made of straw and liked it" sorta way. Leslie was a living Hypercolor sweatshirt.

Our whole family had flown out to California for her funeral, where we sat in pews listening to Whitney Houston's "I Will Always Love You" play out in its entirety. Later, at the post-funeral gathering, my then-eleven-year-old brother, decked out in his navy-blue suit, choked on a piece of roast beef. Nothing says sadness like watching your dad give your brother the Heimlich maneuver as people gently weep nearby.

Leslie was a beloved member of our family, my grandparents' daughter-in-law and mother of their grandson. But she, too, was rarely mentioned after she passed away. The grief and sadness seemed simply too painful for my grandparents to touch. When my mom clocked in as their second daughter-in-law to die, it all felt incredibly unfair. They'd been like daughters to my grandparents, who now had to process their own sadness while also watching their sons and grandchildren anguish. It took me years to even ponder how this must have felt for them, two people who were better at swallowing their grief than discussing it. My esteemed, professional conclusion is that it must have sucked, big time.

My mother was hurt by their silence, taking it to mean that they didn't care. But ultimately, I think their silence meant that they cared an incredible amount, so much so that it was too painful for them to even say the words.

And she, too, approached her illness with a quiet solitude, retreating into her introversion as the disease progressed.

There was no steady stream of visitors into her bedroom, no hordes of people gathered around her. What lifted her spirits was being left mostly alone. Even the idea of having an open funeral overwhelmed her, so she made sure we knew it should just be her immediate family. No close friends, no one on my dad's side of the family. She wanted as little attention as possible, in life and in death.

The silence, the quiet, the desire for privacy above all else—these were foreign and strange tendencies that baffled me, your run-of-the-mill, attention-hungry, slightly insecure loudmouth. This is the perplexing thing about family: you share genes, you have the same unibrow and weird extra-long second toe, and yet the way you manage your grief looks nothing alike. I grew irritated with my mom's quest to be left alone and my grandparents' inability to communicate. But eventually, since she was dead and they were old, my brother became my next target. He was an introvert like my mom, reserved and measured. I was a natural-born talker, and therefore built for therapy and improv comedy the way his long limbs were built for soccer. Even though it took me a while to put words to the sadness I felt, I eventually became very good at flopping down on a chair, tossing a check in my shrink's face, and unloading for forty-five minutes straight. And I didn't stop there: I wrote endlessly about my grief; I called my dad regularly; I emailed long missives to other women with dead moms. Saying the words—"mom," "died," "cancer," "more wine, please"—over and over helped me process my new reality. Naturally, I found every possible opportunity to nudge my brother to make the same decision. This was my role as his pushy big sister, after all. But his consistent refusal to join me slowly brought my irritation at his silence to a bubbling rage.

"You're in pain, and you need help!" I screamed at him one night when we were both home visiting my dad, about a year after she'd died.

"Kate, I don't process things the way you do," he said, his voice firm.

"You're not processing it at all!" I could feel the skin on my neck sizzle off my body in frustration. Why wouldn't he just do *exactly* as I instructed? Didn't he understand that if he just *talked* about my mom's death, he'd feel better?

Instead, he yelled back. "Do you even know what I've done? Do you know that I learned all of *Wildflowers* on guitar?" Oh fuck. I hadn't known this, because my strong suit was clearly yelling more than it was listening. "That's my therapy," he said, storming out of the kitchen.

Of course it was. Of course my brother would work through his grief in solitude like my grandparents and mother had done, teaching himself an entire Tom Petty album on guitar. Talk therapy was of no use to him, and clearly I needed to spend my next few sessions working on how to empathize with him a little bit better.

As we moved forward into Dead Mom Territory, our immediate family unit struggled to figure out how we fit together with a giant piece of us now missing. Losing my mom was like someone chopping off my leg and then insisting I walk just the way I used to. "What's so hard?" the world seemed to be saying as I hobbled along. But for my family to operate together, it was even trickier. We were a stack of Jenga pieces, and the universe yanked out our stable bottom from beneath us while insisting we stay in the same formation. And while there were things we discussed—burial arrangements, funeral readings, who was going to wash the dishes—some topics were simply too painful to put into words. Mainly, how we were going to move forward now that we were permanently changed.

What is it like to be a family unit for so long and then lose the constant thing that connected you, grounded you, made you whole? My family, once on such a clear path, now felt like a group of sailors on a boat returning to a port that had suddenly disappeared.

"Ahoy! Where do we park this thing? The docks are gone. The city, too."

"Let's just keep circling around out here in the ocean until we figure out what the fuck to do!"

"Into the storm? Those clouds look scary! And the waves are choppy."

"I don't know, Jerry—you figure it out!"

"Screw you, Ted!"

Perhaps magically, my family had always been in balance. Two men, two women, two parents, two kids. My dad and I were needy extroverts who craved hugs and were constantly finding new ways to manage our anxiety (him: meditation, me: Xanax); my mom and brother were stoic introverts who were happiest when the house was quiet and they were alone. Then suddenly there was just one woman, one parent, one introvert. Each one of us was left to fend for ourselves against the other two.

The Sunday after she died, my dad and brother were deep
into some football game, two lumps of human form spread
out on the couch and sandwiched between faded throw pillows. I sat in a nearby rocking chair, fuming that neither of
them had even asked if this was what *I* wanted to watch on
TV. I was a combination of pathetic clichés: a woman who
hated football and someone so self-centered that she could
make something as stupid as TV watching all about her. But
in the past my mom and I would have teamed up to insist on
a channel change, or wandered into the living room to dis-
cuss something important, like the cashmere socks featured
on Oprah's "My Favorite Things." I was crushed by something
much bigger than just the boredom I felt watching Tom Brady
hunk it up on the field: the family scales were now tipped, and
right then I was stuck firmly on the one that weighed less. I
wanted to say something, to explain to them how unfair and
awful everything felt. Instead I hugged my knees to my chest,
pressed my lips together, and watched. Suddenly I was the one
staying silent, the one internalizing my sadness and frustration
rather than blabbing it for the rest of my family to hear. In that
moment, I couldn't find the words to say every awful feeling
curdling in my stomach. I couldn't simply say what we all felt:
I was so, so sad she was gone.

As time ticked on, we all took turns feeling left out. When
she died, she left our family collectively behind, but she also
left three very different relationships that existed in three very
different ways. She left my dad after thirty-four years of marriage that took them across the country and back, to brick
houses in New Hampshire and cockroach-infested apartments
in New Orleans, but always together. She left my brother just

as he was becoming a man, a real live adult with a job and an apartment, but still with that sweet, boyish face. And she left me, the indecisive, emotional, panic-attack-prone woman-child who still desperately needed her mom there to tell her exactly what to do.

It took me a long time to realize that just because my brother doesn't reply to my text messages right away doesn't mean he loves me any less. And conversely, that my incessant texts aren't meant to stress him out but to show love. Meanwhile, my dad just had to learn to send a text message without signing his name at the end of each one. ("All of human nature can be explained by our texting habits." —Albert Einstein)

Without her, we had to do the work to get to know the parts of each other that previously only she had known. And conversely, we had to reveal them, too, whether in our words or our actions. It was in accepting these parts, whether we understood them or not, that helped us become whole again, in our grief, and with each other.

FAMILY: A MEDITATION PRACTICE

At some point in my twenties, when I was eating a lot of chickpea stew and not much else, I took a medita-tion workshop. The focus was on loving-kindness and cultivating it in your meditation practice. Sounds sim-ple enough, right? I rolled up to my silk pillow, plopped down, and prepared to bestow unconditional love upon myself. Bada bing, bada *boommmm*.

Our meditation teacher began the class and explained the process: we'd be focusing our meditation on bestowing kindness on ourselves (done), a person we love (easy-peasy), a person we don't know well (The dude in my office mailroom? Sure.), and someone in our life who was difficult (I'm sorry, what?).

It was, as I'm sure you can imagine, a downright pleasure to sit there and wish peace, goodwill, and equanimity upon myself. I mean, who is more deserving of these things than *yourself*?* Even my mailroom dude was no sweat. But visualizing someone I straight-up fuckin' hated, and shooting loving meditation brainwaves in their direction, was T-O-R-T-U-R-E. And yet! There was also a littttttttttttle, teeny-tiny moment there where I experienced a drop of newfound empathy for them. A small drop. But a drop.

Plop.

So I surprised myself when I started implementing this practice in my own life. Not a full-on, daily meditation practice, mind you. I'm not, like, a *good* person. But I did begin to take a second to wish goodwill upon the occasional loathsome person. And it was eye-opening and oddly empowering, as if I were able to take a breath outside of myself and actually consider the world from someone else's point of view. Turns

---

* I *might* be self-absorbed.

out, when you push aside ill feelings and dig way deep in yourself, back behind your guts, to find love to offer up, your perspective shifts. My point? There's no better people to try this with than your family. So the next time some blood relation does something that makes you smack yourself in the face, take a deep breath, dedicate five seconds of loving-kindness their way, and see what happens. Maybe nothing! And that's fine; you just took a deep breath, and that only helps you. But at best, you might find you feel less frustration and more calm. And who doesn't want that?

7

The Holidays

Despite our bickering and communication struggles, there were no other people I'd rather swap coffee breath with on Christmas morning than my family. There was never any doubt in my mind that we'd soldier through the holidays together, fighting the onslaught of Dead Mom Feelings that pop up the second the oldies station switches over to Christmas music. But I also knew that things had to be different because, well, they were different now.

"I don't think I can do Christmas like we normally do," I wrote in an email to my brother, the summer after our mom died. "Yeah," he replied, which was his answer to most things I said because he:

1. Is a man.
2. Is, as previously mentioned, an introvert.
3. Has been dealing with me, a person often described as "a lot," since his very first second on earth.

He and I were both moving through our grief in different ways but were clear on one thing: there was no way in hell we were going to be able to celebrate Christmas the same way we always had without our mom there.

Please allow me to me be very blunt: when it comes to Christmas, my brother and I are spoiled shits. You know those asshole kids who have Christmas presents stacked so high they touch the top of the tree? That's us. And it was all our dear mom's fault. From the moment she bought us Christmas stockings the size of an NBA player's entire leg, we were doomed. She wasn't quick to indulge us on the other 364 days of the year, but on Christmas there were presents that spilled out of our stockings and onto the floor, gifts to open even before we got to the pile of presents under the tree.

But our last holiday season with her was anything but magical, fluctuating from bittersweet to downright nightmarish. She had been living with cancer for over five months when a scan taken in early November showed that, while the tumors hadn't shrunk, they hadn't grown either. This, in the terminal cancer world, is good news and left me feeling stupidly optimistic that maybe she'd be part of that magical 5 percent of people who live for five years with stage four pancreatic cancer. But life was about to drop a big, fat "nope" in my face.

The awfulness started when, a few days before Thanksgiving, she woke in the middle of the night with a fever of 105, my dad racing her to the hospital. She was rushed to the ICU, in septic shock and with a collapsed gallbladder, the combination of which should have killed her. That's what the doctors and nurses quietly muttered to us over and over that week, as she slept in her hospital bed, propped up on a thousand marshmallow pillows. Resting on the bed next to her were two long bags, attached to her stomach by thick tubes. Bile drained from her liver and gallbladder and slowly collected in the bags, brown like rich soil.

"How long are you going to have to have those in?" I asked her one night in the hospital, eyeing the bags precariously.

"I think forever, Kate," she snapped, tired and annoyed. She turned her head to the window, her voice low. "I want to be alone," she said. I bit my lip, a failed attempt to stop the sting of tears. As I wandered out into the endlessly bleak hallways of the ICU, it became real: there was nothing after this. The cancer wasn't just here to stay; it was here to destroy her and our family, too. A holiday gift, with love from cancer.

The one thing more depressing than spending a week lurking on the Intensive Care floor, where people die on the hour, is spending that week in the ICU during a holiday. While many families in America sit in their overheated homes, passing out with pie-filled guts in front of football games on TV, there's a whole other world existing inside the hospital, where it's as if the holidays as we know them do not exist. There are no empty whipped-cream bowls on the counter or Christmas carols on the radio that mingle with the sound of someone washing dishes, lulling you to sleep. It's nothing but death and sadness, a world where families sob openly in waiting rooms because grief very quickly erases any social habits we've formed about emoting in public.

My brother, the one person in our family who genuinely enjoys cooking, had been planning our Thanksgiving menu— right down to a pureed version of things just for my mom, who could not digest solid food anymore, thanks to her tumor. It would be perfect, recalling the Thanksgiving feast we enjoyed for years at our grandparents' house, complete with vegetable lasagna and my grandfather's special rebaked potatoes. I had been desperately looking forward to the meal, because it would signal that things in our family were still *totally* normal. Look at us, a happy, stable, definitely not freaking-out family, celebrating Thanksgiving as if nothing is wrong! Instead, the day before Thanksgiving she was moved out of the ICU and into a regular, not-gonna-die-today hospital room, so we dragged in faded wooden chairs from the waiting room and circled the small coffee table to attempt a half-hearted celebration. We spread out the cornucopia-themed paper tablecloth that our dear neighbor had kindly dropped off, along with some pumpkin pies and cornbread. There we sat, shoving cold cafeteria turkey and gravy into our mouths with plastic sporks as she watched from her hospital-bed perch, taking small bites of green Jell-O. This über-depressing meal was the first sign that things were irrevocably different because of the cancer. I guess I should have been thankful she was out of the ICU, but I was too busy reeling from the realization that we could no longer simply pretend that my mom was not in the depths of dying.

Her health continued to deteriorate into December, but at least we were able to celebrate Christmas at home, away from the blinking screens and endless nurses' visits in the hospital. True to form, she managed to pull off one last decadent Christmas gift haul even in the midst of dying. With the power of internet shopping and her dedicated friends digging through the finest malls of the outer Boston suburbs, my brother and I—two grown adults—still opened a mound of gifts as she lay on the couch, hooked up to an IV drip, too exhausted to even open her presents.

We had gifts under the tree, and we still had her. Like I said, we were *very* spoiled shits.

Once she died, there was no way any of us were going to be able to re-create the magic she spread during the holidays, nor did we have the energy to move through our usual Christmas routine as if nothing had ever happened. She was the one who did it all anyway: she baked the cookies and prepped the chocolate roll and made her regular dish of chicken Marbella and scalloped potatoes. She bought all the shrimp cocktail my grandfather and I shoved in our mouths two hours before dinner started. We just showed up and grifted off of all her hard work. Left to our own devices, we'd surely spend the night sitting around the dining room table taking turns licking the cheese flavor from a packet of Kraft macaroni and cheese because we all forgot how to boil water.

So I made it my mission to plan a family vacation over the next Christmas holiday, something we'd never done before. We weren't much for vacations; we normally spent some weekends in the summer on a lake in New Hampshire and crashed at various grandparent-rented condos in Florida during spring break. This was finally our chance to break into the high-powered world of Families Who Go to the Caribbean for Christmas™!!! We might be morbidly depressed during the entire thing, but hey, at least we'd be tan.

What is it about the Goddamn holidays that makes the grief so much worse anyway? Every single day without your mom is a void, and there are constant, year-round reminders that your mom is now gone. (One whiff of someone on the subway wearing her perfume—Dolce & Gabbana Light Blue—and I'm a mess.) But the holidays hold so many memories—good and bad*—that even the smallest, strangest thing can send you spiraling. Just one stanza of "Grandma Got Run Over by a Reindeer," and I'm suddenly jetting back through time, reliving my entire childhood with her: seeing *The Nutcracker* while wearing scratchy tights and a fur muff, the extended family gatherings every December at the weird buffet restaurant in Copley Place, the Christmas carols that played twenty-four hours from the black boom box on our living room floor. I can feel everything: the warmth of the station wagon, the sound of my parents talking up in the front seats, the eerie darkness of Boston rushing by along the Mass Pike. These are the comforting, throwaway moments that, when repeated every winter, become permanent creases in our memory, folded into the pages of our lives.

How strange it is then that time, set on repeat like this, can move so fast. How odd that our brains latch onto these dull, forgettable moments—the lulls in between life's big events. That these are the times we cry for, long for, that make us ache.

There was no way that we would be able to make it through Christmas sitting in our old spots in our living room,

---

* Okay, fine—mine are not *bad* bad. Mine are bad like, when I was nine, I asked for a keyboard for Christmas and instead my brother got one.

waiting for my mom to bring out the apple cake she made for breakfast each year. It was settled, then. We had to get the hell out of town.

I quickly discovered that most vacationing families plan these things over a year in advance, because by the time I got around to trying to book our trip, almost every resort south of Washington, DC, was full. I tried St. Thomas, Puerto Rico, the Dominican Republic, the Bahamas—every hotel with a beach and a bar by the pool was sold out. The only hotel room still left—and seriously, I mean the only one—was at a Marriott Resort in St. Kitts. God bless this hotel. I say a prayer of thank you to it every day for not being booked to capacity when we needed it the most.

The hotel was your typical, well, Marriott Hotel: really nice but ever so slightly worn. Giant and airy, with pink and blue hues to match the sky at various hours of rising and setting. Chipped paint told the story of the brave, flip-flopped travelers who had walked this path before us. Families bustled through the check-in line in herds, like pasty white cattle. Nearby, sunburnt vacationers sauntered in and out of the casino doors with giant plastic cups of booze, their hands wet from the moisture on their glasses.

Around six AM each day, the lobby filled with moms in visors and lululemon pants, fresh from their workouts. These women were on a mission: early-morning warriors who held coffee in one hand while spreading seventy-eight towels over as many pool chairs as they could find with the other, marking their territory with stiff, white cotton. I had *never* seen this done before. See, the one other time our family went to a beach resort, I was but a pasty fifteen-year-old whose

experience "laying out" was limited to spreading my Dunkin'
Donuts beach towel (free with a box of Munchkins!) along
some dinky New Hampshire lakeshore. On that fateful first
day in Florida, I naively lathered myself in SPF 4 baby oil,
popped Dave Matthews Band's *Under the Table and Dreaming*
on my Discman, and cooked myself like a rotisserie chicken
for eight hours. I came down with a case of sun poisoning so
bad that I had to spend the rest of the week holed up in our
room, fighting chills and a fever while wearing my mom's pink
cotton sweat suit. In short, I was way out of my league.

My family of newbs was no match for these vacation
experts, so we ended up banished to the less desirable beach
chairs, where I read the final Harry Potter book and watched
the same family from New Jersey get hammered on rum cocktails every day before lunchtime.

At night, we bunked together in one room, taking turns
rotating between the two double beds and the cot by the window. Each night my dad would snore gently from whatever bed
he was in, and my brother and I would tease him about it in
the morning.

Surprisingly, the trip was *fun*. But while it was sometimes
easy to escape missing my mom on a Caribbean island, at others it felt as if she were baked into every moment. Even the
most innocuous things seemed to scream "MOM!": the sand
crushing beneath my feet, the endlessly warm sun, the wind
slicing and dicing my face. My brain found ways to work her
absence into every moment. *What would it be like if she were
here?* it asked, as I peeled my thighs off the hot plastic beach
chairs or shoveled Yoplait yogurt into my mouth at the breakfast
buffet. And so the entire week teetered on the edge of darkness

and light, with one foot stuck in I Want Her Back, and the other tentatively sticking a toe in How to Go On Without Her.

In the happier moments we laughed, went for luxuriously long beach walks, and chugged martinis together at the bar. On one of our first nights, my dad began moving to the beat of the steel drum band gently banging out reggae tunes in the lobby. He held his arms in the air as if he were dancing with an invisible partner. "What's he doing?" I asked my brother, who rolled his eyes.

"You need to ask him," he said, and turned his attention back to a TV airing a basketball game from the States.

My dad, a goofy, slightly awkward man who had never once demonstrated an ability to even hear rhythm (he spent years beating our station wagon steering wheel like a drum along to Steve Winwood songs), was suddenly gliding around the floor with ease, his hips tipping back and forth like a scale. Before I could ask what the hell was going on, he grabbed my hand and yanked me toward him, twirling me as if we were the second worst couple on Dancing with the Stars.

"Guess who's going to be ready for our father-daughter dance next summer?" he asked, teasing me.

I stopped and stared at him. "You?" I asked.

He stopped, too, slightly out of breath. "I've been taking dance lessons," he declared proudly, holding his arms open at his side as if to say "TA-DA!"

"For how long?" I asked, genuinely surprised. We spoke almost every day on the phone, and this was the first I'd heard of it.

"Six months," he said. "I wanted to be ready for your wedding."

I turned back toward my brother. "Is he serious? I haven't heard anything about this. "

He nodded. "Oh yeah. Guess who's been hearing all about it?" He pointed at his chest.

I turned back toward my dad. "I wanted it to be a surprise," he said, clearly proud of himself. "My dance teacher is going to choreograph something for our father-daughter dance."

I pushed my lips together, my go-to move when trying not to cry. "How did you even figure out where to go?"

"It was the strangest thing," he said. "I was cleaning out your mom's desk, and there was this business card for dance lessons. She had never even mentioned them to me."

"And so you went."

"I needed something else to do," he said with a shrug. I nodded, thinking of the hours spent counting my Weight Watchers points. I got it.

A few days later, we re-created our most cherished Christmas tradition. Every year, my dad hides a couple of small presents for each kid around the living room on Christmas Eve. The result is a holiday scavenger hunt that still happens each year. Yes, I am a grown adult who still gleefully digs behind bookshelves for presents. And proud of it!

At the hotel, he tucked presents into hiding spots in the lobby, and my brother and I scrounged under faded couch cushions and behind planters the size of our bodies to find our presents as shirtless, sunburnt dad-bros looked on from the bar. As someone who is easily shamed by the judging glances of strangers, I normally balk at doing anything weird in public. But this was our family's *thing*, and no shitty, life-ruining pancreatic cancer was going to stop us. Somehow, in the midst of our pain, we were still us.

When I was growing up, my mom would stand in her apron and watch as the kids tore up the living room, my dad standing next to her grinning, proud of his handiwork. And while it was nice just to feel like our old selves again, it also felt like something bigger, a reminder that despite her enormous influence on our lives, we'd also be okay as a threesome, too.

But our happy moments existed within a cocoon of sadness. There was no escaping our grief. We *were* our grief. I tried to do my crying while in the shower or washing my face at night, or when diving into the arms of the ocean. And we bickered often. One night my dad and I went back and forth, arguing about whether we should wait to eat at a crowded outdoor lobster shack for dinner. We stood there in the sand, snapping at each other and analyzing the crowd, until suddenly, without warning, my brother stormed off. I made a face that resembled a less-cute version of the grimacing emoji. "What's with him?" I asked.

My dad shrugged, and so we followed my brother to where he was stationed near the edge of the water.

"Are you okay?" I asked.

My brother was in tears. "I just don't think she'd want us to be fighting," he said, visibly pissed off at our childish antics.

We shut down our debate about the long wait for dinner and spent the rest of the night quiet and extra gentle with each other. And the lobster was delicious.

One of the most common conversations I have with other Dead Mom people is "How the hell do you get through the holidays?" And while "Escape to the Caribbean!" is a fun answer to give, it's not reasonable to assume most people can combat grief with vacation. I definitely would not have been able to had my father not picked up that hotel bill. (Thank you, Dad.) And the truth of it all is that no matter where you run off to, no matter how you avoid them, or change your traditions, or mix things up, or cook something different, she's still gone. My mom was just as dead when I was on an island in the middle of the ocean as she was when I sat on the toilet in my apartment.

We returned to St. Kitts for our Second Annual Christmas Without Her, but by the third year we were ready to attempt things back at home again. They were different and weird, but nice, like meeting your cousin's new boyfriend after her divorce. I found myself surprised at how good it felt to be back in a known space, to see the old, familiar decorations, to touch the glass ornaments she wrapped so diligently in tissue paper every January. When she first died, I wanted to do everything in my power to avoid her memory at the holidays. But as time ticks on, it's become a season of remembering her. My dad is still hiding presents (for grandkids now, too), and I attempt her apple cake, though it's always a little dry. And there are new traditions, too, things that are just mine: lasagna for Christmas Eve dinner, terrible cartoons we watch with our kids each year.

Was going to an island to get through the holidays nice? Oh hell yes. But it didn't solve things. Running from your grief doesn't actually allow you to avoid it, as much as you hope it will. It just gives you a new, beautiful place to cry in. So yes, give yourself a holiday escape plan, be it a trip around the world, or a new recipe to try, or an HBO binge-watch instead of present-opening. Find your own island, and visit it when you need. When you come back, your grief will be waiting for you, like that one present left unopened under the tree.

GETTING THROUGH THE HOLIDAYS WITHOUT HER: A PLAN THAT MAY OR MAY NOT WORK, BUT FUCK IT, IT'S WORTH A TRY

1. Cook something new.
2. Play board games.
3. Donate all the money you would spend on presents to different charities.
4. Attend a religious service.
5. Take a road trip.
6. Volunteer!
7. Go out to dinner.
8. Go to the movies.
9. Binge watch a TV show as a family. *The Walking Dead* might be too on the nose, but maybe *The Sopranos* could work?

10. Invite over as many random people as possible and host a potluck.
11. Open presents on Christmas Eve, and spend Christmas cleaning the house.
12. Dog-sit for a friend.
13. Take a yoga class.
14. Go for a hike.
15. Start a new tradition.
16. Run or walk a 5K.
17. Plant a tree.
18. Go to a sporting event.
19. Attempt a vegan Thanksgiving.
20. Cry. (What? Crying can be new!)

8

Motherf**kin'
Mother's Day

Of all the holidays you have to endure as a motherless human, Mother's Day is the pinnacle. The worst. The Darth Vader of holidays. So of course the first holiday I'd have to tackle without her would be *Mother's Day*. Contrary to what people say, the universe does *not* have a sense of humor. It's just an asshole.

There I was, twenty-seven, motherless for only ten weeks and in the middle of a process I like to call "returning to your old life after living through your worst nightmare." Every day was a slog that ended with me crying somewhere: waiting on a subway platform, splayed out on the floor of a yoga class in savasana,* or curled up in bed as sleep eluded me. The looming arrival of Mother's Day only heightened my depression. My mom died in early March, and the ads for Mother's Day switched on only a few weeks later. It was impossible to eat a

---

* Which is, ironically, known as corpse pose. Thanks for nothing, yoga.

pint of Häagen-Dazs while watching CW reruns, or track all
those Weight Watcher points on the internet, without bump-
ing into some sort of ad for Mother's Day flowers or Mother's
Day jewelry. Every person going through their first motherless Mother's Day soon realizes that every single store on the
planet is out to get you with some sort of Mother's Day sale.
You could buy a Mother's Day baked ham if you wanted. (And
I do! Honestly, that sounds delicious. Nothing says "Dead
Mom Grief" like salty meat.) Every kiss begins with Kay, and
it turns out, so does every hysterical weeping Mother's Day
meltdown.

I was desperate for a distraction, something to focus on
besides the gaping, mom-shaped hole in my life. When I came
across a 10K race for kidney disease that just so happened to
be on Mother's Day, I pounced. I knew nothing about kidney disease (sorry, I am sure it is awful), but something about
pounding my bones against hot concrete felt right—as if I
might just be able to crush myself up into oblivion and forget
the entire day.

Instead, training for the race just gave me more time alone
with my memories of her. My brain circled back over and over
to one Mother's Day in college, when I drove the three hours
from Maine to surprise her at brunch outside Boston. There
she was at a table with my dad and brother, looking as stately
and graceful as ever, despite the lack of air conditioning so
desperately needed on that abnormally hot May day. Our eyes
hit as I walked in, and she jutted her head forward in surprise
before standing, arms ready for the hug that was to come.
When our bodies finally connected, I could see that she was
crying, and something about that reaction made me feel so

proud. I couldn't believe that my mom loved me so much that my appearance in a mediocre suburban restaurant serving dry eggs and cheap champagne could move her to tears. As I ran, I saw that moment—her shocked face, her standing to hug me, her smile and wet eyes—over and over again.

But what haunted me even more during my runs was not being able to remember how I'd celebrated her last Mother's Day alive. I could not recall what I'd done to mark the day— probably a phone call or a voicemail left in haste. I went back and dug through old emails to see if I sent a note or an e-card, but there was nothing. On race day, I stomped along the running trail of Central Park in tears, furious with myself for not showering her with balloons and flowers and gifts to demonstrate how much she meant to me, how much I would miss her when she was gone.

The next few Mother's Days without my mom felt awkward and stiff, like shoving yourself into a new pair of jeans—the terrible, no-stretch kind!—that are two sizes too small. One year, two of my close friends invited me out for brunch. It was an incredibly thoughtful gesture, their way of protecting and standing by me on a tough day. But it just made me irritated and annoyed—how could they possibly think I could handle brunch on Mother's Day?—and so I declined. Another year, I hid in the back row of a yoga class filled with adult women and their moms and sobbed. Unbeknownst to me, the studio had offered a deal that day—bring your mom to class, and she gets in for free! A great deal for everyone, except those of us who had gone to yoga class in an attempt to hide out from Mother's Day for ninety minutes. I couldn't fault the frugal moms around me, but their presence was like being punched by the universe.

What I've learned is this: there is no getting around Mother's Day. Every year its looming arrival causes an emotional explosion. One day in early April, I'm minding my own business, buying some cheese for my book club, when suddenly an email pops up on my phone. Crate and Barrel has "fresh gift ideas for mom!" And there I am, standing in line at Trader Joe's, spiraling. No matter what I do—I set up ad-blockers to avoid the endless barrage of Mother's Day content online, vent in my secret Dead Mom Facebook group, avoid brunch—Mother's Day still shows up and sticks its middle fingers in my face. I, for one, am sick of it.

And so, my dear fellow motherless humans of the world, I am here to announce that the time has come.

We are taking back Mother's Day, damn it.

Our days of feeling nauseous come mid-April, of avoiding TV ads and the card aisle in Target, are over. No longer will we cringe at the families lined up for brunch or the bouquets of overpriced flowers we have no reason to buy. This is our day, too, and it's time we owned it.

Look, I'm not claiming to be the best at getting through this annual DEFCON 1 shitstorm of emotions. But these years of working through my Mother's Day issues have led to a new way of doing things. At some point, a couple years ago, I grew tired of the dread and depression that appeared every Mother's Day. The misery and pity I put myself through every May is exhausting, and I reached my limit. It didn't seem fair that the day stopped being mine simply because I didn't have a mom with whom to celebrate. I want a day, too, for fart's sake.

So instead of dragging my depressed, lonely self through another month of Mother's Day misery, I started asking myself

WWYMWYTDOMD? (That's "What Would Your Mom Want You to Do on Mother's Day?" in case acronyms aren't you're thing.) I do not know your mothers, but if they're anything like mine was—a total queen with a drawer full of headbands and very old L.L.Bean wool clogs—here is the answer: she wouldn't want you to cower or mope, to avoid the sunshine and the spring and the world around you. She'd want you to honor her not with some schlocky, faux-sentimental bullshit. She'd want you to kick Mother's Day in the ass and then make out with it. She'd want you to have a fucking wonderful day. The best day. One she'd love to hear about on the phone at night while she simultaneously watched Wolf Blitzer, cooked dinner, and snapped at you to "stop cussing so much, jeez."

It's simplistic, sure, but the truth is: nothing can change the fact that our moms are dead. My mom is dead! (Try screaming this out loud some time. It will feel good and scare that one asshole neighbor who always looks at you weird.) The only thing that can change is us, the living humans left behind in death's wake. And as stupid and commercialized as the holiday is, there's no stopping the Mother's Day machine as it chugs along. Mother's Day is here to stay, and, Beyoncé willing, so are we.

So how do we share space with what is arguably one of the worst days of a motherless person's life? It's simple, but it's also so damn hard. We must do Mother's Day differently. That's it. This year, go out and have the day you'd want to have with your mom if she were still alive. For me that means I'm going to drink tea with too much sugar, listen to *Car Talk* in the kitchen, and head to Bloomingdale's to spend too much money on La Mer face cream. I'm going to get a pedicure, splurge for the ten-minute foot massage, and not feel guilty that someone has to touch my leg stubble. I'm going to post every old photo I have of her on every social media account I have, including my long-dead MySpace page because you can never have too much of My Mom. I am going to buy myself a bouquet of flowers and shower myself with the love I'd give to her, if only she were here.

And dammit, I'm going to spoil my daughters, too. I have two wonderful tiny humans, and I take neither of them for granted. Since coming into the world, they have filled my Mother's Days with incredible joy and also atrocious but adorable handmade Mother's Day artwork. They are excited to celebrate me, and let's be honest, *I* am excited to celebrate me. If you saw the amount of pee I cleaned up off the floor every week, you'd celebrate me, too.

Is Mother's Day still hard? Duh. Yes. Someone else should be celebrating with us, too, but she died years ago, and I simply can't comprehend the unfairness of it all. But when my sadness starts creeping in, I get out my megaphone and scream, "Not today, Satan!" And then I explain to the strangers walking by me on the street that by Satan, I mean Mother's Day, and they give me a weird look and scurry off. I'll call that a victory.

Mother's Day doesn't have to be just about honoring the living. But it doesn't have to be about the dead either. It can be about honoring *you*, because you are one of the best things she ever did (and if for some reason she never told you that, I am telling you so). You deserve to have a Goddamn great day whether she's here or not, whether you are a mom or not, whether your mom was deserving of every Mother's Day gift or not. Now it's up to you to use Mother's Day to mother yourself: nurture yourself; be kind, tender, and loving to your needs. Treat yourself. Start new, weird traditions that make the day joyful again. Arrange a Mother's Day gift exchange with other people you know who suffer on this day, too. Volunteer your time; go rock climbing; split a bottle of wine or five with the other motherless friends in your life.

Celebrate the person you've become not just in her absence, but because of it. Don't just get through the day— own it, for fuck's sake. Some of the most magical moments in my life occurred as my mom was dying: our relationship strengthened; I felt the true kindness of friends and strangers; I learned I'm a lot tougher than I give myself credit for. This is the painful, beautiful truth about grief that only those who have been sucked into it can understand. Happy things grow from sadness, and Mother's Day is no different. Find the small speck of joy in an otherwise bummer of a day. And let it grow.

THE DEAD MOMS CLUB MOTHER'S DAY GIFT EXCHANGE BONANZA TO HELP YOU FEEL BETTER ON AN OTHERWISE CRAPTASTIC DAY!™

- Wake up on January 1; realize that Mother's Day is fast approaching. Shudder. Go back to sleep.
- In March, check in with your fellow Dead Moms Club members. This is as simple as emailing the one other person you know with a dead mom and

saying, "Hey, do you want to exchange gifts for Mother's Day so we feel less miserable? And do you know anyone else with dead moms who might want to join?" If you do not know anyone else with a dead mom, you at least know me, and I am easy to stalk via Google.

- If you are arranging the gift exchange, pair members, and send out names and addresses by April 1.
- Set your gift exchange parameters. This means that everyone but celebrities and billionaires should cap the spending limit at around $20.
- There is a hard rule against Edible Arrangements. Seriously, who can eat all that fruit?
- Make sure gifts are in the mail by May 1, to reach Dead Moms Club members by doomsday, Mother's Day, which is held on the second Sunday in May.
- Don't stress too much about it. This is meant to be fun, and seriously, just a little note sent through the mail is a serious day-brightener.
- If you really have no idea what to send, might I suggest the two-pound tub of cheese balls I just found on Amazon for $14? No one's gonna be mad about an actual tub of salty, artificially flavored snacks that can be easily tossed into your own mouth.

9

Your Newly Single Parent

My mother was adamant—to me anyway—that she wanted my father to date and remarry after her death. She joked about it often, when we were waiting for her acupuncture appointments or driving home from chemo. "When your dad has his new trophy wife," she said, "make sure she doesn't take down all the pictures of me."

"Mom," I scolded. I was still enjoying my life in Denial Town, where my mom's stage four cancer was magically beatable and we'd both live forever. I did not do well when she mentioned a future without her in it, even if it was just a joke.

But she also discussed the possibility of my dad remarrying in a serious, no-nonsense tone, and I knew she meant it with every fiber in her frail, ailing body. She loved him, and that meant she loved him enough to want him to be happy again. "Your dad's young," she said anytime the topic came up. "There's no reason he shouldn't get married again."

"Sure, sure," I nodded along, biting the insides of my mouth to keep myself from screaming. "Of course."

Honestly I would have said or done anything to keep her feeling at ease and happy, and to allow her to die in peace. *"What's that, Mom? You think* Grease *is superior to its sequel* Grease 2? *Oh yes, you're so* right about that one." Anything to make her feel a little joy in the middle of the cancer hellscape in which we were trapped.

So if that meant acting as if I were cool with my dad dating again, then *fiiiine*, I'd act cool with it. But the truth was that the thought of him romantically holding hands with another human besides my mom—much less marrying one!— sent me looking for the nearest trash can to hurl in. I very naively assumed my parents would die holding each other in a bed basked in soft, natural light like those old people in *The Notebook*. Now, I also once assumed I'd at least have a shot at boning Ryan Gosling, so obviously I was not a human operating on a plane of reality. But my parents had been together since they were wee college fresh-people, and the most awe-inspiring thing about their thirty-four-year marriage is that they genuinely still liked (and loved) each other. Their relationship was affectionate, playful, and supportive. Each night my dad would come home from work and tromp upstairs to change out of his suit, and my mom would follow so they could hang out in their bedroom and break down their days like true partners. They almost never fought in front of my brother and me—and were so good at keeping their issues from us that I didn't even know they had any conflict until I was well into my twenties. They were tender and loving, leaving each other love notes and cards on a regular basis. (Once my mom had the nerve to tell me that they were still "intimate" until her cancer diagnosis. This is both admirable and enviable, and also the grossest thing I'd ever heard.)

There was no way I could ever replace my mom. And so I let this logic seep into my feelings about my dad remarrying, too. I wasn't going to ever get a new mom, so why should he get a new wife? I wasn't going to go out and court new moms over coffee and museum dates, so why should he? My dad was fifty-four years old when my mom died, and as far as I was concerned, his romantic life was now over. He had a good run! High fives all around! Time to hang it all up and call it a day. And that's the end of that.

Now look, I am 110 percent on board with people remarrying, be it after divorce, spousal death, or mysterious disappearance à la Olivia Newton John's boyfriend.* But things enter a different dimension when you throw your own parent into the mix. What sounds like an obvious and wonderful life choice for someone else feels terrifying and life-ruining when it's your own dad, especially when you're a selfish and scared adult-baby like me, who couldn't imagine her parents brushing their teeth next to someone else, much less sharing a life with that person.

So you can imagine the internal meltdown I experienced when my dad informed me that he had started asking women out on dates. We were seated across from each other at an Italian place in my hometown, about four months after my mom died. It was a genuinely good time despite the lingering

---

* *You guys.* He faked his own death. He is living in Mexico right this very second! Google it when you finish this book, and enjoy your trip down that crazy rabbit hole.

Dead Mom Depression; there was laughing, imbibing, and I had saved up enough of my Weight Watchers points to eat all the dinner rolls, since my dad doesn't "do" bread. A solid night! And then, suddenly, a bombshell.

"Wuh yuh suh?" I asked through a mouthful of sourdough.

"She's nice," he said. "I met her at a conference we had for work."

I nodded along, playing the role of super-supportive daughter who wants to know every OMG-worthy detail. But inside, my brain was a fireworks show. He continued, "She has two kids, who are seven and eleven." I reached for my glass of wine and violently emptied its contents into my throat like someone dumping out a trash can. And then, in my slightly buzzed haze, I got real with myself. *Kate*, I said silently, as one does when conversing with one's own mind, *you can either act like a piece of shit ingrate and make this all about you, or you can support your dad, who is a good human being with a semi-decent head of hair and a lot of love left to give someone.*

I begrudgingly went with the latter. And I ordered another glass of wine.

Since my mom's death, my dad and I had already been talking almost daily, two needy chatterboxes filling the Mom-shaped void in the other's life. But that night officially marked a shift in our relationship, from father-daughter to two pals gabbin' about romance. Soon our conversations shifted to your typical generational debate over online dating (I thought it was a great way to meet people; he refused) and the details of his romantic pursuits. This new side of our relationship left me feeling both awesome (Go, Dad!) and really, really weird. His happiness—which I wanted for him so badly—threatened to change everything in my life. This was a new, strange kind of internal conflict, and one that required a level of selflessness that was, if I am being honest, very hard. Because at my core I was scared, terrified of new change on top of the still-fresh change of life without my mom. But also I feared some movie-caliber monster stepmom barging in, brainwashing my dad, throwing out my mom's things, and breaking up my family.

Even weirder, I was possessive. I didn't want to share the one parent I had left. If I could have locked my dad in an attic, *Jane Eyre*–style, I definitely would have. As I said, I wasn't particularly good with being selfless when it came to wanting what was best for my dad.

Much to my relief, Conference Woman faded out of the picture, too busy with young kids and her job to date much. *Good riddance to her!* I thought, wiping my hands clean like a villain in an '80s movie. But soon after, I got a call from my dad. He had met a woman in a bookstore, essentially living out the plot of *You've Got Mail*. He was browsing cookbooks to buy for my brother for Christmas, and they'd started chatting. She recommended *How to Cook Everything*, which he dutifully bought. They'd hit it off, and she'd mentioned the company she worked for, but he hadn't gotten her name. Would it be weird, he asked me, if he called the company, described the woman's appearance, and asked the receptionist to connect him?

"YES," I shouted into my phone. "Unless you want her to think you're a middle-aged Ted Bundy." He did it anyway. She did not take him up on his offer of coffee.

In his defense, what a miserable experience it must have been to be thrown into the dating world at fifty-four years old. The last time he was single, he was seventeen and fresh off a road trip to Woodstock. You have no agency when it comes to the death of your partner—you are stripped of them, and your life together, in an instant. So he'd earned the right to date around while his adult kids kept their mouths shut and dealt with their conflicted emotions about it. I marveled as he asked women out with zero insecurity or expectation or fear of rejection—he put himself out there over and over again because his desire for human connection was that pure and genuine. I was proud of him, honestly. His hustle was inspiring. But still there was a part of me—a selfish, monstrous part—that felt the sweetest sense of relief every time one of his attempted love connections fizzled.

"I met someone," he said one night about a year after my mom died, his voice zipping through the phone line with audible excitement. "She takes the dance lesson right after mine." His voice shifted to boastful. "I asked her out, and she said yes!"

I knew the second he told me this that something about this woman was different. It wasn't just how excited he was; it was that it sounded as if *she* were into him, too. A few days later, he called to report back on their first date, at an Asian-fusion restaurant near his house.

"It was great," he said, sounding tired but pleased. "She came back for tea, and then we talked all night."

My entire body began night-sweating even though it was the middle of the morning. Was my dad telling the truth, or was he using the same half-lies I dropped on him and my mom when I went out with my high school boyfriend years ago? I mean, we all knew what "talking all night" entailed, right?

I gently pried the G-rated details out of my dad: she was a doctor, born and raised in Northern Ireland, who also competed as a ballroom dancer. "She's beautiful," he cooed. "And so tall!"

These were the first things I ever learned about my stepmother.

It took me weeks to build up enough courage to Google her, and when I finally did, I had the help of some happy hour cocktails to spur me on. I found her on her hospital's website, a member of the pediatric radiology department. She had a huge, welcoming smile and looked like a red-haired Tilda Swinton (a comparison I have since mentioned to her and she may or may not like, I'm not sure).

The challenging part about juggling your emotions while grieving is that rational and irrational thought can coexist together. I *was* genuinely overjoyed by my dad's happiness. His mood improved; he seemed lighter, livelier, and most importantly, he had someone to do things with again. After my mom died, I had the luxury of returning to my old life in New York, while my brother started a new one at business school. We could escape and surround ourselves with sounds and smells that had nothing to do with our mom. But my dad was there in our old house, the one they'd lived in since 1986, trying to start a new life while still walled in by her clothes, her books, and the unending silence that comes with living alone. The last thing I wanted him to be was lonely. But the thought of him having a girlfriend made my insides twitch. I was fine with the abstract idea of it, but the reality of it stunk, like being Dutch-ovened with the worst fart ever.

Fortunately, my dear father, a kind man who obsessively reads newspapers and pronounces the letter *h* silently, had the patience of a saint who was quickly losing his patience. He would not invite his new girlfriend to my wedding, he agreed, after I aggressively shut down the idea. But, he told me one night over the phone, exasperated, "you're going to have to meet her eventually."

And so the happy couple planned a trip to visit me in New York that fall. I prepared for it like any normal person would: I spent my entire week's paycheck on a new outfit at Bloomingdale's consisting of a brightly patterned Marc Jacobs top, J Brand corduroys, and a purple shrug. It was a terrible investment, as none of these clothes fit me now. But I desperately wanted my dad's new girlfriend to like me, even though I had already decided I didn't like her. She'd done nothing wrong, of course, except be the person he chose to date.

I struggled with accepting my dad's new relationship because it was—*terrible pun alert*—the final nail in the "Oh, my mom really is dead" coffin. Nothing solidifies the eternal absence of your mom quite like the moving on of her devoted, adoring husband.

Welcoming a new person into the fold of your already shifted and morphed family can be incredibly challenging. I'd be lying to you if I claimed to have handled the introduction of my stepmother with grace or an open mind. Her existence terrified me, my own personal Babadook. I met her arrival with fear, plain and simple. "YOU ARE GOING TO CHANGE EVERYTHING IN MY LIFE AND I DO NOT LIKE IT!" I wanted to scream.

It wasn't that I worried she was going to replace my mom. But her arrival signaled a complete shift in every angle of our rebuilt family dynamic. Families are, essentially, one big inside joke, and now we had a new person in the mix who didn't get the references or know the punch line. She didn't know who normally does the dishes after dinner and who stands around and wipes the countertops over and over, pretending to help (that's me, folks). She didn't know that we fold the towels in thirds or that when I was a kid we ate Mexican food every Sunday night. The interloper throws off the equilibrium of things. My mom's death had been unsettling enough. But we'd adjusted to our life without her, our "new normal," so much so that I was in no mood to embrace the new, new normal that had just walked in.

The first time I met her, I could not understand a single word she said. Okay fine, I maybe got "Hello," and "I'll have the pork ragu." But her Northern Ireland accent was no match for my obtuse, uncultured American ears. Processing her words felt like jamming a fish into a straw: they just didn't fit into my ear holes.

Instead I sat quietly across from her at a table at a loud downtown Italian restaurant, nodding along to whatever she said to make it look as if I were comprehending her words. And even though my ears could not keep up, my eyes were on top of things. It was clear just by watching his body language that my dad was into her, or in the words of late-aughts pop culture sensation *Jersey Shore*, he was DTF. (Dad, please don't Google this.) Watching them together was like sitting across from two teenagers in love for the first time: it was both adorable because *yay, love!* and slightly horrifying because *ew, love.*

The strangest part of our first meeting was that I never once considered that she might be nervous or scared, too, until she said so, with a hearty laugh, years after they were married. And then it all dawned on me at once: how awful it must have been for her to try to ease her way into a tight-knit family still clinging to the memory of their gone-too-soon mom. She had to plod through the yuck of our decades-old drama and crack our familial code as my brother and I watched on with judging, skeptical eyes.

This is not a task for the faint of heart. But she kicked ass at it. She was patient with our hesitancy, kind whenever we invaded her and our dad's space. She welcomed us into her home and cooked us elaborate, expansive breakfast spreads, with pancakes sprinkled in powdered sugar, tomatoes roasted perfectly in the oven, and eggs poached just so. She figured out who did the dishes after dinner and how we folded our towels.

My stepmom, with all her delightful quirks (she packs five suitcases for a weeklong trip, is almost always running late, and can mess up your kitchen like nobody's business), handled the whole inheriting-adult-children-and-their-flaws thing with the grace of Jackie Kennedy. And it wasn't just to get us to like her—she's genuinely a decent human being. Imagine that! She still gamely attends Thanksgiving each year with my *mom's* family (and enjoys it!). She's never once tried to erase or overpower the memory of our mom, and instead happily coexists with her—pictures of my parents sit alongside photos of my stepmom and my dad. She's never forced her presence or attempted to overreach into our lives. She's an incredible, attentive grandmother to my children and goes out of her way to make time for them. She answers all my frantic "You're a doctor—can you tell me what this mole is????!!!!!" text messages with kindness and speed. She is always down for an in-depth discussion of One Direction.

But what really mattered is not how she went out of her way to be awesome at stepmomming. It's that she is, herself, an awesome person. And over time I began to know her not just in relation to what she did for me, or how she adjusted to our family, but simply for who she is. It took a few years, because I'm occasionally a self-absorbed troll in size Tall jeans, but when I finally looked beyond my "me bubble," I could actually see *her*: kindhearted, endlessly generous, and with an aversion to movies with foul language. I admire her fearlessness: she left her family farm to attend boarding school at just eleven years old, went to medical school, and then moved to the States, which is seriously badass. (Meanwhile, I do not like going to any other Starbucks besides my regular spot.) She's proud, and stubborn, and has a booming, hearty laugh my ears are addicted to. She's a seasoned ballroom dancer who maintains a separate room full of bedazzled gowns reserved for competitions. She doesn't just deal with all my dad's weirdness (stacks of months-old newspapers that he slowly reads, for example); she *likes* it. It turns out, adding a new member to our family didn't throw everything off balance. It stabilized us. But best of all, she gave my mother the one thing she wanted, something the rest of us could not deliver: a loving, supportive, and joyful partner for my dad. And for this, I am forever in her debt.

THE SUPER QUICK, TOTALLY UNSCIENTIFIC STEPPARENT TEST

I know watching a parent with someone new can leave even the most chill person feeling squeamish. So I've put together a quick and easy list of qualities to look for—and avoid—in your new stepparent. This is based on my expertise as a human with emotions and feelings who likes to judge people, and nothing more.

DOES THIS PERSON RESPECT AND HONOR YOUR RELATIONSHIP WITH YOUR LIVING PARENT?

Correct answer: YES. A good stepparent, IMHO, will support your relationship with your surviving parent and give you two the space to let it grow and evolve without interfering.

DOES HE OR SHE KNOW WHAT HEALTHY BOUNDARIES ARE?

Correct answer: YES. Marrying into your family does not give anyone the right to go too deeply into your space—be it personal, emotional, physical.

IS THIS PERSON KIND TO WAITERS AT RESTAURANTS?

Correct answer: YES. This is an unscientific but very accurate way to glean if someone is a dick. Pay attention to restaurant manners! Check out how they speak to people in the service industry. Analyze the tips they leave. This is a window into the soul!

DO THEY HOARD ANIMALS?

Correct answer: NO. I dunno—this just seems like a pretty universal red flag.

⟶

10

Being Motherless

I was twenty-eight when I realized something very important about myself: I had no idea how to cook rice. Not paella, or a rice casserole, or even some fancy-schmancy rice, like jasmine or basmati. I simply had no clue how to cook the blandest, most basic member of the rice family: plain white rice.

For something so simple, my questions were endless. How many cups of water do you need per cup of rice? Do you boil the water first and then add the rice, or dump it all in together and let them do their thing? How long does rice cook for? What even *is* rice, anyway? A carb? A grain? Does it come from a plant?

It should've been the easiest cooking exercise in the world, yet there I was in my tiny galley kitchen with the tacky blue Formica countertops, holding the cheapest bag of store-brand rice I could find, with zero idea of what to do with it.

I reached across the counter for my phone. Instinctively I opened up my Favorites and found my mom's name, still standing strong in the number one position ahead of my dad, my brother, and the twenty-four-hour diner across the street.

But instead of hitting her number with my finger, I stared at it until my eyes shifted cross-eyed. My little brain chugged along, trying to keep up. *Oh, right,* it remembered. *You can't call her, ya dummy. She's dead.*

This urge is more than just a habit. For most of us the desire to call our moms with a question, or thought, or exciting or terrible news is etched into our muscle memory. For my whole life she was there if I was sick at four in the morning in college or crying in a bathroom stall at work. She sat and listened to countless rambling, angst-filled "What am I doing with my life?!" calls as I wandered the loud streets of New York, walking to and from work, comedy shows, and empty bars. She was there, she was there, and then—she wasn't.

How strange, that our bodies know to reach out for them, to call for them, even when they've been gone for years. In my email account, under Sent Messages, there is an email I wrote and sent to my mother, dated six months after she died. The subject is simply ".". The message is blank. I don't remember writing or sending it, but there it is, a call into the void, an attempt to still find her even though I knew that she was gone.

Here's the problem with being motherless: you never really accept it, no matter how many years it's been. Sure you can intellectually comprehend that your mom's body is no longer walking the earth, leaning over the kitchen counter dipping her tea bag in and out of that mug you gave her that one year for Christmas, or finding great deals at her local Target. She is gone—you know that. You get it. And yet. You can never completely shut off that part of your brain that hears a great bit of gossip about your childhood best friend's brother and thinks, "Oh shit, I gotta call my mom."

Part of living life without them is constantly searching for them. It's why your heart skips a beat when you sit behind a woman on the subway with the exact same stick-straight, salt-and-pepper hair. The world is filled with Almosts, people who could *almost* be her, if only. And so you move forward in life: strangers become friends, a semi-famous person retweets you on Twitter, and your grief starts to dissipate a little. But the need, the longing, the pull toward her—it never goes away. There will always be moments when you start to reach for her, and you must remind yourself over and over: "Oh right, she's gone. She's *gone*." How is it that my life can grow so much since her death, and morph into this pulsing, vibrant thing that stumbles along and thrives, even with a hole in it the shape of a five-foot-eight woman wearing J.Jill jeans and a flowy Eileen Fisher top?

The first time it hit me that my future was going to be motherless, I curled up in my bed, wailing. She was still alive, newly diagnosed with cancer and attached to machines in the hospital. It was the day after my brother and I got the call from our dad about her diagnosis; we drove from New York City straight to the hospital in Boston. We spent that day lingering around her bed, dividing our time between crying and teaching our dad how to text message. (It was 2006, such an innocent, emoji-less time.) But there was nowhere for us to actually sleep in her hospital room, so we left our dad to battle it out with the pullout chair and drove back to our childhood home. The second we got there I raced upstairs, flung myself into my old double bed, and just . . . let it out. At some point my brother crammed himself in next to me, still so young and boyish at twenty-three, and performed the very awkward job of comforting his inconsolable older sister. In between excreting the most snot ever made by one human's nose, I listed all the things she was sure to miss: My wedding. The birth of my kids. The day Britney and Justin inevitably get back together. The thought of her not being there for these things seemed unimaginable, unsurvivable. Andrew kept reassuring me, "It's going to be okay," but I was adamant: I simply could not—*would* not—move through the world without her. You're reading this book, so I'm guessing you know how well that plan worked out.

If you've lost your mom, chances are friends, family members, and other parents have offered to "help." I was overwhelmed by the people who stepped up for me in my life, who made sure I knew that they were there for me if and when I needed. But I had no idea how to actually ask for it. Does this make me a troubled, confused human? Absolutely. I have diagnosed myself, thanks to many internet quizzes. But every time I thought of asking someone for help with something—*anything*—the thought of it paralyzed me. The things I needed help with seemed so silly and embarrassing (Can I put clothes that say "hand wash" in the washing machine?!) that I always ended up avoiding human contact, Googling my questions, and shrinking my clothes anyway.

Remember that rice I didn't know how to cook? I did not call my dad, or an aunt, or a friend. I did not consult my number one BFF, the internet. Instead I just tossed it in the trash and ordered Chinese food. In the end, it wasn't really about the rice at all. It was about wanting her back, wanting her there in the ways I'd had her for so long.

The first time I tried to force another person into the role of mom, it was a tiny disaster. It had only been a week or so after mom died, and my whole family was in that weird place of having nothing to do now that our main activity was dead. When you caregive for so long, it becomes the only thing you know how to do. Even the simple act of sitting down to watch TV feels foreign and strange. But I had just received an email from my soon-to-be-married friend Susan, asking her bridesmaids to pick out a black dress to wear in her wedding. I had what my life coach Oprah describes as an "aha" moment. As in "aha, here's something that will get our asses out of the house." I cornered my dad as he sat in front of the computer, looking at his work email. "Hey," I said, making my pitch. "I need to go to Bloomingdale's to buy a bridesmaid's dress for Susan's wedding. Can you come and help?"

My dad is a man of style. I say this without a hint of irony—he actually has lovely taste in clothes. There are no hacky golf shirts or giant white sneakers in this dude's closet. His suits are always tailored to perfection and spruced up with suspenders, colorful ties, and quirky cuff links. In the '80s he somehow made wearing bolo ties with collared shirts look cool. (He did go through a short phase where he obsessively wore jam pants, but we'll let it slide.) He even enjoys shopping. And so he gamely agreed to accompany me to the mall for some dress hunting. But did he have any idea what shopping for a dress in an upscale department store with his daughter, who was eager to cure her grief by maxing out her already maxed-out credit card, would entail? No. No, he did not.

My mom had been my lifelong shopping buddy. As a kid she bought me Laura Ashley jumpsuits in blinding floral patterns and my first leather jacket. Later, in my broke twenties, she'd pick up the tab on dresses I couldn't afford, never flinching when I sheepishly walked to the dressing room with armfuls of clothes. But the most important stuff was not the items themselves (though they were really nice—thanks, Mom); it was the time we spent together, laughing, chatting, and bonding. Were she alive, she would have been the one sitting next to me in the driver's seat, speeding down Route 9 toward the mall.

The second we walked through the giant glass doors of Bloomie's, I knew my grand idea for a recovery shopping trip was a mistake. I immediately began searching for a Big Brown Bag to hide in. Everything about the department store— and the mall attached to it—seemed to pulse, like one giant migraine headache. I glanced over at my dad, whose face was affixed in a horrified, squinting grimace. It was as if we were both tripping on mushrooms: the lights were too bright, the walls too white, the music too loud. Ladies hawking perfume distorted into melty shapes; Boston grandmothers shuffling along in their driving moccasins and barn jackets dissolved into blobs. It was then that I realized the awful truth: we were not ready to exist in the outside world yet.

At home, we were safe in our grief bubble, where we ate takeout eggplant parmesan and watched *Deal or No Deal* and cried quietly in our own rooms at night. This weird, outside world where "normal" people existed was overwhelming and enormous, and so obviously void of her. I wanted to climb atop the Clinique counter and shout, "How are you all just walking around and shopping like nothing happened?! Don't you know my mom just died?! Don't you understand that I can't do this without her? ARGHREIHAHR!" (That, of course, is the sound of me throwing a hundred Happy perfume bottles in the air.)

But I'd forced this situation on us, so I put on a game face that looked more like a pained frown. I moved through the dress section, grabbing anything that looked black and wasn't pants. Arms finally full, I marched us to the dressing rooms, pointed my dad toward a chair, and slammed the dressing room door shut. I slid into one of the dresses, haltered it around my neck, and paraded out to show my father, who was sitting, legs bouncing, in a giant gray chair. "Nice," he said. "You ready to go?"

"What? No, I came out here to show you the first one." We stared at each other.

"It looks great," he said quickly. "Are you going to get it?"

"Dad," I said, my voice returning to its irritated, teenage roots. "I have, like, a mountain of dresses to try on."

"Okay, well, I might just go wait in the car," he said, clearly miserable. I turned and stomped back to the dressing room. Shoving my dad into the role of my mom was a failure, and so I stuffed my legs back into my pink Forever 21 sweatpants (iconic and classic, lemme tell you) and walked out silently, the dresses abandoned in a pile in the dressing room.

My dad is an amazing father who has stepped up for me every second of my life. This is a guy who took me to countless Red Sox games and never made me leave early, who patiently toured colleges with me even though I was not speaking to him at the time (for no good reason, if I remember correctly), who once drove an hour to bring me my wallet that I'd left at home after embarking on a road trip to visit a friend in Pennsylvania. I had just turned twenty-one, and he knew that my need to drink legally in college bars was of the utmost importance. He is stellar in every way, but he was not my mom.

Sometimes I would dream of finding a sixtyish-year-old lady friend, someone who enjoyed going out for tea and listening to me judge my peers purely out of jealousy for their more fabulous, put-together lives and careers. I formed strange, maternal crushes on women I hardly knew. I watched them in Trader Joe's or on the subway and wondered if perhaps they, too, were longing for a one-sided friendship with a daughter figure who demanded unbridled attention and unconditional support on the regular. Unsurprisingly, I had no takers.

I became obsessed with a gray-haired woman who frequented my yoga class, rushing in late with her bike helmet clasped in her hand, her arm stacked with silver bangles. I would try to smile at her, even drop some eye contact her way, and she always gave me a nod of acknowledgment. We worked our way up to a real live yoga-class friendship, where you greet the other students you recognize with a hello, maybe toss them a block or two from time to time. *It's happening!* I thought to myself one evening after class as she said good night to me in the elevator before unhitching her bike from a lamppost. I was on the verge of asking her to coffee, when one day I heard her mention her daughter to our teacher. "She's coming to class with me tomorrow," she said, excited. I froze, overheated with jealousy. I then instantly felt weird and ashamed about my reaction. I had claimed this woman in my head, like some sort of telepathic platonic pickup artist. But our relationship was more fantasy than fact: I didn't even know her name. I was just another friendly, sweaty face she saw a couple times a week. I bolted out of the studio and never looked in her direction again.

I attempted to cobble together a replacement mom, leaning on a hodgepodge of friends, relatives, my mom's friends, and social media. But it didn't quite do the trick—it was like stacking three kids on each other's shoulders, shoving them into a giant overcoat and a wig, and having them pretend to be her.

But my biggest challenge arose when Anthony proposed to me in a whiskey-induced frenzy at a Tribeca bar in front of a small group of our best friends. I know I've mentioned this wedding and this fiancé a couple times already (he's now my husband, so it all worked out!), so let me be clear: this happened in June, just four months after she died. Cooking rice was one thing, but planning a wedding without my mom felt like a nightmare, an unsolvable task made even more miserable by her absence.

You know those women who love every second of wedding planning? Who relish the little details, dream of their dresses, handmake the name cards, and grow the miniature pine trees that they later hand out as their parting gifts? Cool, now imagine the opposite of that and mix in an anxiety disorder, with a healthy dose of fear of disappointing people. Top it off with the stench of Dead Mom Grief. Voilà! It's *me*.

She was supposed to be there for my wedding, Goddamn it. Not just to have some sort of magical mother-daughter bonding experience (though that would have been nice, of course), but to force me to do all the mundane crap I did not want to do. I needed her there to yell at me about deciding on seating arrangements and to remind me to send thank-you notes for all the nice Crate and Barrel plates we received.

Planning a wedding so soon after her death meant that every element of it was tinged with grief.

In short, I had *a lot* of panic attacks.

So imagine my surprise when my dad, who just a few months earlier had barely been able to sit for fifteen minutes in a reasonably comfortable Bloomingdale's dressing room chair, called me up to tell me that he wanted to come wedding dress shopping with me.

"What?" I'd said, shouting into my phone in the middle of a bodega, where I was piling tofu curry into a container the size of a shoe box for dinner.

"I want to come dress shopping!" he said again, his voice eager and excited.

"Dad, it's going to be boring," I said. "My girlfriends can take me."

"Kate." He sounded irritated that I wasn't getting it, like when he used to try to teach me fractions with sticks of gum. "It'll be fun—we'll make a weekend of it." He paused. "And your brother wants to come, too."

And that's how I ended up standing on a platform in the middle of Kleinfeld Bridal at nine thirty in the morning as my best friend, Liese, my dad, and my brother sat smushed next to each other, thigh-to-thigh on an ice-white couch.

"I like it," my brother said as I rotated in a backless lace number, moving carefully as if the dress were made of bees. Next to him, Liese nodded approvingly, as was her job as maid of honor/very attentive best friend.

"I don't know," my dad said, shaking his head so that his glasses fell down his nose. "I like it, but it's not the one."

And my dad, with his hands on his khaki-clad hips, fingers hooked around his suspenders, was right. It was gorgeous and stately, but not totally it. And so off we went, crisscrossing the city via subway on the hunt for a dress. Every time we entered a new bridal salon, I'd introduce my party to the doe-eyed, perfectly coiffed salesperson behind the counter. And each time their eyes would roam the faces of my group, searching for my mother. I watched their brains work in real time as they checked off each face: *Friend, check, brother, okayyyy, hmm, this must be her dad, sooooo, no mom. Okay, got it.* Still, it was as if these people had never seen a motherless woman before. This odd reaction quickly buoyed my father and brother's presence into a source of pride for me. I got so good at anticipating the salespeople's reaction that by the end of the day I would introduce my group and then lower my voice and say, "My mom just died," just to see what they'd do. Most of the time they offered me extra champagne.

Later that afternoon, inside a quiet bridal shop, I found the right dress. I loved it, with its simple heart-shaped neckline and buttons down the back, with a bow that hung right over the spot of the tacky butterfly tattoo I got at nineteen. I shuffled out of the dressing room, the sample dress pinned tight around my waist with binder clips. My dad nodded, pushing his bifocals up his nose to get a better look. "Oh yeah, Katie," he said, using a nickname only my parents were allowed to utter. "That's it. That's the one."

And he was right. It was even more perfect not just because I loved it, but also because the people who had come to support me loved it, too.

I gave him a hug. "Thank you," I whispered, because my voice was on the verge of cracking. "You know, for coming with me and stuff."

He nodded. "I wouldn't miss it." He gave me a squeeze. "Now," he said. "Can we go?"

I waddled back to the dressing room to change, and as I slipped off the dress, I realized then, standing there in nothing but a corset and underwear I bought at the Gap when I was in high school, that I didn't need people to fill her shoes. They were unfillable, after all. I just needed people to walk beside me in their own way.

So often people mention our dead moms as a way to offer reassurance: "She would have loved the dress," "She would be so proud," "She'd think you were beautiful," "She's with you in spirit." But that day, my dad never mentioned my mom once. Because who the hell knows what she would have thought? She's not here. And I am motherless. But I am not peopleless.

About fifty times a day I tell my daughters to "use their words" when they want something. But what they don't know is that it's taken me years to figure out how to do that, too. Asking for help hasn't come easy to me; even now it feels foreign to take the questions I'd lob at my mom and toss them to someone else. The ways in which mothers are just *there* is endless, so much so that it feels foreign to heap those questions and problems on someone else.

But I tried. I called my foodie friend Teresa for cooking help in the throes of a pregnancy craving for red meat. I was a confused and ravenous vegetarian holding six ounces of filet mignon in my hand who needed iron and had no idea how to make this hunk of flesh edible. She called in support from her own mom, and together—over the phone—they helped me fry up the best steak I'd ever eaten. And when I finished my meal, I felt full. Not just of delicious, perfectly pan-fried meat—but of confidence and calm. Who knew a quest to grill steak could be such an empowering experience?

The second I realized that (1) asking for help was fairly easy and (2) people enjoyed doing it, I went for it. Slowly I got more confident in reaching out to people. I started texting my aunts, who are now my go-to people for sharing kid pics and commiserating over *Pretty Little Liars* plot twists. My uncles share stories about my mom that feel new every time they tell them. My mother-in-law gives me all her best recipes, cooks for me when she visits, and reorganizes my cupboards and dresser drawers. My stepmom, the doctor, counseled me through pregnancy pains, heart palpitations, and a torn ankle tendon. I keep a running list of broken things in my house and hand it off to my father-in-law to fix every time he visits. My brother is my sounding board for laughing about my dad, my best friend the person I go to to share the political fears I would have texted to my mom. And my dad is who he's always been to me: a dad.

I went from a Too Scared to Ask Anyone for Anything kind of person to a Demands Everything from Everyone sorta gal. And you know what? I like it. It feels nice to lean on people and to offer the same in return.*

It doesn't just take a village to raise a child—it takes a village to raise ourselves. Lean back and let your world carry you, or leap into their arms like you're doing the most daring

---

* Do you want advice on how to organize your kids' toys or which version of *Pride and Prejudice* to watch? Call me!

trust fall at an otherwise boring corporate retreat. They will catch you and hold you up when you're certain you're about to collapse, and eventually they'll walk you over to a mirror and say, "See? You've lost her, but you've got us." Eventually, asking them for help will be the easiest thing in the world. Like cooking white rice.

RECIPE: HOW TO COOK WHITE RICE

Step 1: Open the cupboard and get the rice. If you don't have any rice, give up and order a pizza. It will taste way better.

Step 2: Measure out one cup of rice. Pat yourself on the back because you're really doin' this! Good job.

Step 3: You are now supposed to wash the rice. I've never done this once in my entire life. Honestly, what is the point of cleaning rice when you're about to boil the crap out of it a few seconds later? (Please don't tell me the actual answer. I enjoy this ignorant, self-righteous rice bubble I've created for myself.) Decide who you want to emulate: a classy, clean-minded person who respects the laws of cooking or me, and move forward.

Step 4: Pour two cups of water into a pot. Easy-peasy. Sing to yourself "I take two cups water, I take one cup rice" to the tune of Paula Abdul's 1989 hit song

"Opposites Attract," in which she duets with a cartoon cat. This is an actual thing that happened.

Step 5: If you really want to live on the flavor edge, toss a dash of salt in there, too.

Step 6: Boil the water. Marvel at how long it actually takes for something so insignificant to happen. Become overwhelmed at the thought of time, and how no matter how fast or slow it moves, it is both painful and beautiful. Begin to cry, and blow your nose in a damp dish towel because you forgot to buy tissues. Hang the towel back up. I won't tell.

Step 7: Pour the rice in the water! It's all happening! You're cooking!

Step 8: Give things a stir, reduce to a simmer, and put the lid on the pot.

Step 9: Set a timer for twenty minutes.

Step 10: Wait.

Step 11: Wait some more. Good Lord, this takes a long time.

Step 12: Use these twenty minutes for something productive: fold laundry; unload the dishwasher; pay some bills.

Step 13: Give up on productive activity after one minute; use the remaining time to check Facebook.

Step 14: When the timer goes off, try not to beat yourself up for wasting nineteen minutes on Facebook.

Step 15: Turn off the stove and let the rice sit, covered, for a couple of minutes. Pace.

Step 16: Congratulations! You've cooked something all by yourself! Your white rice is ready to eat.

Step 17: Feel overwhelming pride and accomplishment. You. Did. It.

Step 18: Realize you could have just bought a bag of microwavable rice—or a rice cooker!—and avoided this whole thing. Next time.

11

Seeing Them Everywhere

My mom was propped up in bed resting against a tower of pillows, exhausted. Her own mom had died just a week before, and she was still in mourning, grieving, tears welling at the corner of her eyes as her spindly fingers grasped at the locket around her neck. Inside was the minuscule photo of my Gramy Betty's face, so tiny and sweet, framed by the soft gray hair she pinned up the same way every day that I knew her.

"I just miss my mom," she said, her voice hoarse.

"I know, Mommy," I said, both because she had said this to me numerous times over the course of the week and because I could relate. I missed my mom, too. Sure, she was still here, right in front of me in her Garnet Hill pajama set, but oh, how I already longed for her and our old life together.

We had just started hospice for her in our house. A few days prior my parents had returned home from their meeting with her oncologist, defeated. The chemo was not working. She lay out long on the couch, still wearing her velvet winter hat. "I tried," she cried as I sat next to her on the floor, rubbing her arm. "I did."

"I know, Mom," I said. I attempted to hold it together for a second before I starting weeping along with her.

"I want to keep fighting it," she said. "But there's nothing else I can do." She crossed her arms, frustrated and defeated. So many well-intentioned people had encouraged her to "keep fighting," but it was impossible advice. Terminal cancer isn't a football team that the underdog can eventually topple with a coach's pep talk about clear eyes and a full heart. It is the Terminator of illnesses, the one that won't stop until it annihilates every healthy cell in your body because that's what it's been programmed to do.

Everything awful that could have possibly happened to my family did so all at once, like the third act of a sappy Lifetime drama. My grandmother died, her body finally giving in to old age. Then just a couple days later, my mom landed back in the hospital, her stomach once again blocked by her growing tumor. The scans showed that the cancer was spreading all over her liver at lightning speed, the new spots on her scan taunting us. "And you thought chemo would work! Idiots," they seemed to say. Hospice felt like defeat; even though she was still alive, it was over. I felt like the person who leaves a baseball game at the bottom of the eighth inning because there's no hope of the home team winning. She was still in the game, but she had already lost.

So as she lay there in her bed, sniffling back tears over my grandmother, I knew what was coming. I could escape into my denial, but the truth was, I had started grieving her death the second the cancer showed up and crashed our lives like a drunk hotel guest who plows into a wedding during the last dance.

Though I am mortified to admit it, my mother's grief over her own mom's passing made me quietly furious. Obviously, her sadness was justified. Her own mom had just died, and she was terminally ill. This is, to put it nicely, a nightmare. Who wouldn't be deeply despondent over the death of a parent, no matter the age or circumstance? Loss is loss is loss; I understand this. But my rational mind had wandered away from my brain months before, and all that was left was raging, selfish, animal emotion. It made me wild with anger that she had the audacity to be sad about her mom, who eked out a solid ninety years, while my whole world was falling apart because she— my own mother—was about to die at just fifty-six. My mom got to have her mom for her whole damn life! And here I was, about to be motherless at twenty-seven. How could she not see how unfair things were for me?

My grandmother had been a pivotal figure in my life, and I loved her something fierce. But I was so destroyed by the deterioration of my own mother that I barely even felt a blip of sadness at her passing. It was as if someone had entered the information into my brain, "Your grandmother has died," and pressed enter. Instead of processing it and reacting appropriately, I just became one human color wheel, spinning forever until I needed to be shut down and rebooted. If anything, watching her die after such a long and fruitful life only highlighted the brutal unfairness of my mom's swift and random illness.

Look, I know what you're probably thinking: *Kate sure is a real asshole to be angry at her dying mother for grieving her own dead mom.* And you're right! My behavior was horrendously selfish, childish, and insensitive. God, I'm mortified by it. It's more cringe-y than a YouTube video compiling the most embarrassing Oscar acceptance speeches of all time. I have no good excuse for it. But at the time, the unfairness of it all left third-degree rage burns all over my insides.

I had just come upstairs to refresh my mom's water with another tiny Poland Spring bottle. (She liked them ice cold, so we'd freeze them and let them melt at her bedside, removing them the second they lacked ice.) But a simple water switch had turned into that tear-filled moment, as seemed to be the norm in those days. At any given moment in our house, someone was crying. It was all we seemed to do. Cry; give her an Ensure smoothie; cry; help her walk to the bathroom; cry; give her some more Oxycontin; cry. When someone you love is in the final stages of death, you get so good at crying you don't even need a specific thing to cry about. Just glancing at a cucumber on the kitchen counter can spiral you down a weepy path: remembering how mom used to cut up cucumbers for my picky brother every night when we were kids + the knowledge that my mom will never be able to eat a cucumber again because of her tumor = an unstoppable river of tears.

That day in her room, she started crying about her mom, and I responded with my own tears, crying about *my* mom. We'd been like this so many times before, wet-faced and heaving together on her bed. I reached for the tissue box on her bedside table and noticed a black beetle on her pillow, slowly crawling toward her head. It was about an inch long and smooth, its body like a wet rock freshly lifted out of a lake. Now, I am well versed in the world of insects (I went to summer camp for eight years, so I essentially have a PhD in Bugs and How to Kill Them), but I had never seen a beetle like this before, with its small body and sharp angles.

"Mom, look," I said, tapping her arm. "There's a weird bug on your pillow."

She pressed her hands into the mattress and shimmied her body up away from the pillows, turning her head. She eyed it quietly before greeting it with a smile, the first I'd seen all week. "Maybe it's Gramy coming to visit me," she said, locking eyes with me. The thought seemed to settle her, and so I grabbed more tissues and scooped the bug up gently, so as not to squash its body. It was February, the earth outside hard and frozen, so I placed it in the bathtub, figuring it could maybe crawl down the drain back to the underworld of insects from whence it came.

Now let me back up a step. My family has a few universal qualities that all members share: we are tall, we like nicknames, and we don't freak out about bugs. We embrace them. We treat them like adopted children, cooing over their extra legs. Growing up, I was the weird girl with the mom who refused to sweep cobwebs off the ceiling out of respect for the spiders who spun them. Instead she nurtured their little homes, draped in the corners of our living room. "I love spiders," she'd declare, swooping in to scoop up the daddy longlegs that sometimes snuck inside our house in the summer. Her tone suggested that anyone who didn't share her affection for them was an idiot. "They kill mosquitos," she'd say with a shrug, her New England pragmatism showing.

But while my mom was merely an insect cheerleader, my grandma was bug-obsessed,* the human ambassador to the

---

* My daughter recently got upset when I told her that we'd have to kill the lice on her head, so clearly this is hereditary.

insect world. She collected beetle carcasses and displayed them on the shelf like other grandmothers showed off Precious Moments figurines. She was nothing like my friends' grandmothers, who wore shimmery tracksuits and exercised by walking circles in the mall with their girlfriends. My Gramy spent her time sculpting her grandkids' heads out of dark, red clay in the pottery studio in her garage and covering walls in her house with paintings of the constellations. She was consumed by nature, books, and art, and spread that love on to us grandkids, who worshipped her. An average day with her involved preserving the skeletons of mice killed by her cat, making prints of leaves in plaster, and listening to the morose cry of loons on the lake as we sat on the steps of her house, plucking the stems off of green beans picked from her garden. After she died, I found a small bag of her cat's whiskers tucked into a plastic bag with a note requesting they be given to my youngest cousin. She was a renaissance woman living in a country town with fewer than 1,200 people, completely unafraid of nature's quirks.

My grandmother's love of the earth's bizarre bounty was passed down to my mom and her siblings, along with long legs and oval fingernail beds. My mom started her own beetle carcass collection alongside a table of Disney figurines I collected as a kid. She regularly reminded me to "feed my birds"* as she lay dying in her bed. Other times she'd jokingly ask us to push her bed out into the woods, so she could just die there with no one watching. There was some truth to her request.

---

* These were, of course, just the chickadees that lived in our yard.

My mom was often more at ease in nature than she was around other people. So of course she thought her mother had come back to visit her in bug form. I believed it, too. My grandmother probably got to the front gates of heaven and was like, "Pardon me, God, but this weird cloud castle is not for me. Can't you just use your God wand and zap me back down to earth as something smaller and . . . *creepier*?"

The beetle disappeared after I dropped it in my mom's tub, and I didn't give it much thought after that. Almost every house in New England is old and dusty, with various bug infestations throughout the year. People shrug when one hundred ladybugs take up residence in the crevasses of a windowsill, so who cared about a little beetle? As my mother's health quickly slipped away from her through the month, I expected the beetle to make an appearance, to show up and really prove that it was my grandmother in a six-legged disguise after all. But she died before it ever returned.

Two weeks after my mom's death, I was spread out on the floor of the family room at our house in New Hampshire. A few hours earlier we'd shuffled into the cold, wooden pews of her childhood church for my mom's very small service, open to just immediate family. Most of us were dressed in all black, but there was nothing glamorous about our fashion choices. I had bought a $30 dress at Target and, because the world was still an icy slush factory, paired it with two pairs of tights and knee-high black Uggs. Anthony had dug up the black suit he'd worn to his own mom's funeral five years earlier. Clearly that suit had had it, because as he sat down in the pew the pants split right up the butt seam. We'd sat in the same spot less than two months earlier for my grandmother's service, and so the whole thing felt like the most depressing déjà vu ever. Normally I would have laughed at his fate—lovingly, of course— but the humor of the moment didn't even register. I was in such a depressed daze that I couldn't even appreciate a pants-rip *at a funeral*. What a waste.

After the service we drove our cars up to the grave site. I whispered hello to my grandmother as we shuffled by her gravestone on our way to my mom's new home. The ground was rock solid and coated in snow, but the cemetery had somehow managed to dig a hole big enough for the urn vault. I always assumed we'd just toss the urn right into the ground, and let the white ashes of her body soak back into the earth. But instead we buried my mom's little urn inside of a small, square box that looked like a coffin meant for a Happy Meal.

The minister's mouth moved, making the shape of words that did not enter my ears. Instead all I could hear was the buzzing of my own brain, the squeal of an amp getting too close to a guitar. She was dressed like a Hogwarts professor in a long, black cloak, and her rainbow reverend scarf* flapped around her neck, making her look like a bird with broken wings trying desperately to get off the ground. Suddenly I felt my dad's elbow jab my ribs through the soft buffer of my winter coat. "Kate?" the reverend said gently, making a face that signaled it was not her first time saying my name. "Oh," I muttered, and reached a hand into my pocket, digging around. "Right."

I had volunteered to read "Do Not Stand at My Grave and Weep," a poem my mom once cut out of a newspaper and taped

---

* I'm sure this has a name. I'll Google it in ten years and let you know.

to her bulletin board in the kitchen years before. You know this poem—it's the one read at *every* secular or Christian-lite funeral. It's the kind of poem that sounds incredibly cheesy and trite, until it's about *your* person. Then it suddenly transforms into the most meaningful piece of poetry ever written. I had read a different poem just minutes before at her service and had shocked myself at how easily the words had flown out of my mouth. But now I stood there, smoothing out the creases of the paper that I'd folded into my pocket with my fat, gloved hands. And I couldn't say a thing. I opened my mouth, but the combination of thinking about her crushed up into ash mixed with the words on the paper in front of me describing her as the wind suddenly caused my entire body to convulse. This was not a quiet, graceful cry, like one Jackie Onassis might have mastered. This was full-on snot-sucking weeping, making sounds like a horse dying a slow death.

My dad finally wedged the paper from my hands and read each word in a clear, slow voice. Then we stood in a shivering herd and cried, as my uncle stood at the bottom of the hill and played "Taps" on his trumpet.

Whew, what a great morning!

It had been what the internet likes to call *A Day*, and we'd all gone back to our house, shoved our mouths full of warm food, and sunken into various spots, enjoying the excessive heat pouring out from the woodstoves, which were all going at full blast. I was on the floor with my cousins, entwined in the sort of cuddle pile reserved only for people who share the same DNA and embarrassing family traits.

"Hey," said one of my statuesque cousins (they are all amazing individuals with unique interests, styles, and lives, but for the purpose of this story please imagine them as a sea of slightly different Gwyneth Paltrows with varying shades of long blond and brown hair). "Look."

She pointed a long finger to a spot on the floor. There, next to her fingertip, were two black beetles. The same exact kind of bug that had appeared on my mom's pillow at our house in Massachusetts just weeks earlier.

Now you may be saying, "Hey, um, Kate—Massachusetts and New Hampshire are basically the same place."* It's not crazy to think that these beetles might appear in both locations. Beetles are, like, the most basic of bugs. The pumpkin spice latte of bugs. And it was winter—they were probably just inside trying to escape the snow.

If you're saying these things: congratulations. You are a pragmatic, reasonable person who will go far in life.

Not me.

See, I took this as a sign that my mom and grandmother were there, with us, delivering a very important message in bug form.

"Hey guys, we're together, and we're fine!" I imagined my bug mother saying as she crawled slowly across the rug. "We've come back to see how things are doing. You know me, always checking up on you. I may be dead, but I'm still your mom. Cute dress!"

The idea of my mom dying and then magically shape-shifting into animal form to visit me was oddly comforting.

---

* Apologies to citizens of both states who will surely bristle at this comparison, but New Hampshire is merely a grumpier, more mountainous version of Massachusetts with slightly fewer Dunkin' Donuts per mile and a way more badass state motto.

Believing that she was simply an insect kinda made it feel as if maybe she hadn't really died at all. Sure she was *gone*, but she was lingering, looking out, checking in on me. It gave me a sliver of peace in the midst of my dark, swirling grief.

So I did what any normal person would do: I lived through the first year of life after my mom's death desperate and thirsty for signs that she was still with me. I wept when bugs landed on my arms. I cooed at the ashy-colored mice that scurried along subway rails. "Hi, Mommy," I sang at every bird I passed on the street, even the pigeons that clung to leaky air conditioners that dotted the outside of apartment buildings and more than once crapped on my head as I walked under them. I didn't care if my mom was that rat dragging a slice of pizza down the steps of the Times Square subway station if it meant she was still the littlest bit alive.

If you thought that my mother being reincarnated as vermin was the weirdest belief I held after her death, think again, friends. Almost immediately after she died, every appliance in our house broke. The whole first week of life without her was spent stumbling on another electrical item that had just randomly given up. The washing machine stopped churning; the vacuum finally kicked it; the microwave died and needed to be replaced. Lights went out all over our kitchen. Coincidence? Maybe. Ghost Mom coming back to teach us a lesson about self-sufficiency? *Hell yes*. And lucky for us, she left us prepared.

Just days after her diagnosis my mom had sat at her desk for hours, scribbling instructions out on index cards explaining how everything in our house worked. She scotch-taped messages all around the house, so that she could gently correct us on what we were doing wrong even if she wasn't alive to do so. On her bedroom window she tacked up a note that read, "*Air Conditioning* *If you look out this window and see water dripping, go outside to see if it is from spout above window. If so, call HVAC.*" She made a list of the different kind of lightbulbs each socket needed. They sat stacked high on the top shelf of our kitchen closet, with detailed notes on which bulb went in what socket. Every time I reached into the cabinet to replace a burnt one, her instructions greeted me, breathing her life back into the air. She went through all her jewelry, organizing everything with notes like, "Earrings and rings from D!* Rings have been appraised." She'd even tacked on a small strip of tape to the container of her expensive face lotion that sat in her bathroom cabinet. "Don't use too much!" the note read. "Only need small dab."

When everything stopped working that week, I imagined her floating somewhere in the ether, testing us from the beyond, making sure we could survive even the most mundane task without her. And even if the various electrical breakdowns were simply just that, with no spiritual influence, she was still there, speaking to us through her scribbled words. She was dead, but she was also right there at every turn: practical, helpful, controlling without being too pushy, but still making sure everything was done her way.

I spent my mom's illness deep in denial about her looming death, but she always knew she wasn't going to make it to my wedding. One night, a couple months before she died,

---

* My parents' lifelong nickname for each other, the origins of which were a secret kept from my brother and me. Hmmm.

she suggested we make a list of all the people who should be invited for my big day. Cousins, my college roommates, family friends I might forget. We sat together on the couch as she wrote the list in slight, slanted cursive, a sign that the cancer was weakening even her strong, steady artist hands. "Mom" is the first name on the list.

When the time came to actually create an invite list, I used this piece of paper like a Bible—inviting every single person we'd named. A hundred sixty-four people said yes, and suddenly, after months of planning tables and plucking hairs and one hysterical, weeping meltdown about the chance of rain, our wedding weekend arrived.

We finally made it to the Friday night before the wedding, and people were walking up the gravel driveway of my dad's house for the rehearsal dinner. It was August, she'd been dead a full year and a half now, but it still felt fresh and recent. I was hiding upstairs in a bedroom, watching the arrivals through the bathroom window while huffing my way through yet another anxiety attack. I was the person who had never once thrown myself a birthday party because the fear that people might have a terrible time was just too much for me to handle. And now here I was, summoning humans from all moments of my life together in a hot, dusty field to eat bacon-wrapped figs together. My heart was performing a drum solo inside my chest.

But Anthony dragged me downstairs with the patience only a person who is set to marry you in twenty-four hours can have, and the party got underway without a hitch. My father-in-law delivered a lovely blessing, my dad referenced my ex-boyfriend only once in his toast, and the wine did its job of acting as a liquid Xanax.

Midway through the evening, I noticed the world's weird-est mix of people standing in a circle off to the side of the dinner tables. Two of my cousins were splayed, legs long, in the grass. A couple of the dudes from my improv group stood nearby. Next to them, my aunt Betsy crouched low, her hands examining something in the grass. It's always a red flag when random wedding guests mix voluntarily, and so I hustled over, wobbling on my size-eleven J.Crew wedge heels.

"Hey guys," I said to the world's weirdest squad.

"Kitty-Kate," my aunt said, her brown eyes wide. "Look what we found."

Nested in the grass were two squirming baby chipmunks. My mind immediately zipped back in time to the bugs, and I knew instantly: these weren't just baby chipmunks. They were my mom and grandmother, crashing my rehearsal dinner.

"I'm going to take them home," she said, and I nodded, smiling. If there was one place orphaned chipmunks wanted to be, it was at my aunt's farmhouse. She was legendary in our family for nursing animals back to health, be it a goat with a broken leg or the baby bird I found outside of its nest when I was four.

The chipmunks put me at ease, comforted me, trans-formed my mood from terrified to on top of the world. I went from a nervous, nail-chewing bride to Oprah on "My Favorite Things" episode day, confident and poised, shouting at every-one in an abnormally deep voice. "You guyyyys," I hollered at the table of my best girlfriends from high school as I sashayed toward them, wine bottle in hand. I had given them each a canvas tote bag as a present, which was more or less the same as getting a new car.

Planning my wedding without my mom had been an emotionally turbulent ride, peppered with angry outbursts over the smallest things. The sorrow I felt over her absence, both at my wedding and in my life, swallowed me. I managed to smile and celebrate and even enjoy my wedding weekend. But my heart was still raw, sandpapered bare by my sadness. And now, just like with the beetles, she was *here*. Sure, she weighed only a pound, and her gray hair was now a striking, unnatural chestnut, but she was here. The chipmunks somehow made everything okay.

The next morning my dad pulled me aside as my bridesmaids sat in our living room, getting their hair twisted into updos. "This is from your mom," he said, handing me an envelope. On the front, in her tiny cursive, were the words "For Kate—On Her Wedding Day." I raced upstairs, locked myself in the bathroom, and blasted the ancient heating fan so no one could hear me cry. I flopped my body onto the toilet seat and tore open the envelope. Suddenly she was here again, alive through her words. The card was short and direct, typical of my mother. But every word still hit me like an emotional wrecking ball. "I can picture how beautiful you are," she wrote. "I am with you in spirit, Kate."

"I know you are," I whispered, weeping on the toilet seat. "You're a bug, and a chipmunk, and the broken washing machine, and you're still here."

With my alternative universe, insect-chipmunk mom at my side, our wedding went off without a hitch. The sun shone, and I made it down the aisle in my heels. Later that night, when word got around that Obama had announced his veep choice, our friends led an impromptu "JOE BIDEN" chant as the DJ played George Michael's "Freedom 90." You know, your typical, normal wedding stuff. There were plenty of forces helping to make sure everything was perfect—my doting friends and family, our hired wedding planner. But in my gut I gave all credit to my mom, in her new spiritual element.

A few years later, at Thanksgiving, I piled a plate with food and plopped down next to Aunt Betsy, who was squashed onto the corner of the couch, a plate of food balancing on her knees as if it were the last piece in a heated game of Jenga. The house was full of family, and we'd joined the stragglers who'd missed out on the actual table seats in the dining room. She asked me about work and life in New York, and when we got quiet chewing, I remembered something I'd been meaning to ask. "Hey," I said, turkey stuck in my teeth. "Whatever happened to those chipmunks you found at our wedding?"

I had envisioned them occasionally scampering in her mudroom, nipping snacks out of her fingers. Maybe she'd released them back into the wild, and every so often she caught a glimpse of them peeking out from behind a stone wall, their way of showing gratitude, saying thank you.

"Oh," she said, squinting her eyes ever so slightly, the sure sign someone knows there's more to your question than just a light, casual inquiry. "They died a few days after I brought them home."

I nodded and played it cool, because on a practical level, I understood that this is what happens to all animals, especially young, wild ones abandoned by their mother. And let's be real: this idea that my mom was now living out eternity as an animal or insect was totally normal inside my own head, but

saying the words aloud to someone—"Oh no, but those chipmunks were my mom and grandmother, reincarnated!"—was
the kind of thing that warrants a gentle, concerned look and
a whispered, "You're in therapy, right?" But inside, my entire
spiritual belief system— mainly that my mom had come back
to life with varying amounts of fur and legs—was collapsing
onto itself. I hadn't told anyone of the significance I'd placed
on all these weird, wild creatures. But I'd simply taken all the
hope I once had that she might beat her cancer and, when
she died, plopped it over onto the idea of her existing in some
sort of spirit world. It was my own way of keeping her alive,
because she was too big, too important, too perfect to simply
just go, to dissolve into nothing, to never come back.

I wanted so badly to believe that my mom was somehow
still with me in animal form that it took me forever to see
that she *was* still here, just not in the way I had once thought.
My mom had written herself alive—scribbled on the notes
she taped to our appliances and in the handwritten letters
she wrote as she was dying. And now, her words are still all
around me, breathing, pulsing, beating. She's here, in pieces,
on paper. But she's here.

Yet still, I see animals everywhere that look bigger,
brighter, completely filled with her. A few weeks ago I sat at a
red light across from my kids' preschool and watched a mother
duck usher her six ducklings along the sidewalk of a busy street
where there is no body of water anywhere close. And this past
summer, in New Hampshire, an enormous, sunflower-yellow

butterfly danced in the air above my kids' heads before landing on a pile of dog crap. *Seriously.* It was the most beautiful, disgusting thing I've ever seen.

Is she there, in the mother duck and the butterfly, making them more vibrant, more alive? Or do I see the beauty in the world more clearly simply because she's not in it?

A few days later on that same East Coast trip, I walked with my family along a pier nestled up against Boston Harbor, as the summer sun took its sweet time setting on the water. My dad walked ahead of me, each of his hands connected to one of my girls. And as I stood there and marveled at the glorious sight of my family and the world around me, a slender green bug landed on my forearm. I looked at it, tears tempting fate at the corner of my eyes.

"Hi, Mom," I said quietly to the insect. "I miss you so much."

And then, without even thinking, I squashed it, and ran to catch up with my family.

———

FIELD GUIDE: HOW TO TELL IF AN ANIMAL IS YOUR DEAD MOM OR JUST A REGULAR BORING OLD ANIMAL

There is a precise formula that goes into my determining if an animal is indeed my dead mom. I've perfected this criteria throughout my ten years of grieving. If you've ever wondered if your mom is living out her afterlife as your neighbor's ferret, read on.

First, are you having a particularly sad, weepy, I-miss-my-mom sorta day? If so, any animal you see is almost definitely your dead mom. On those kinds of days, she's inside of *everything.* Even those gross moths who won't stop invading the cereal boxes in your kitchen. (Just me?)

Next, did the animal poop or pee on you? If the answer is a resounding "GROSS. And yes," then it's definitely a Dead Mom Animal. I know what you're thinking: "My mom was really proper. She'd never do . . . *that.*"

Hate to break it to you, but yeah, she *definitely* would. Do you know how many times you pooped and peed on her as a baby? It's the perfect time for her to execute revenge. A bird pooping on you is already considered good luck—now imagine that it's your mom bestowing that good luck on you. Even better!

Is the animal adorable? Then it's totally your mom. This is a given.

Is it a hummingbird? If so, it's your mom for sure. Every hummingbird is really a dead person in disguise. Anything else is just a regular ol' dumb animal. Including your cat. No offense.

12

Hello from the Other Side

For me, imagining my mother reincarnated as different animals was like a gateway drug to the afterlife. My reasoning was logical(ish)—if my mother was injecting her spirit into beetles, then certainly I might be able to contact her in other ways. So I did the next obvious thing in my quest to find this invisible version of my mother.

I saw a psychic.

Let's get this out of the way, because I know 97 percent of you are already rolling your eyes at me (hi, Dad): Yes, it's true. I, esteemed Nordstrom Rack loyalty card holder Kate Spencer, believe that psychic mediums can talk to dead people. Specifically, *my* dead people. I believe this because, eight years after my mom died, I paid $250 to sit with a psychic in a clinical, bright white office and talk to my dead mom through her.

Go ahead, grimace. Shake your head in pragmatic disgust. I know what you're probably thinking. I've thought it, too! And I know what you're going to say, so let me just stop you now. Yes, I read that *New York Times* story about the psychics who were arrested for scamming that sad British dude out of over $700,000. No, it still didn't change my mind.

In hindsight, I'm surprised I didn't rush out the day after my mom died and drive to the nearest building with a neon "Psychic" sign in the window. It never even occurred to me that this was an option. Rather, the idea landed in my brain in the most millennial way possible: I saw it on Instagram. More specifically, I saw her, my future psychic, smiling widely in a writer's photo feed. This person was someone whose work I'd read and admired, and I took their selfie together as an endorsement; if Cool Writer considered this psychic to be legit, then that was all I needed to hear.*

Look, I wasn't a total idiot. I didn't just find a psychic on Instagram and then throw my money in her face. What kind of person do you think I am? I did thoughtful, measured research: I looked her up on Yelp, and her reviews were overwhelmingly positive. In my book of *Is This Person Reputable?*, it was an open-and-shut case.

Still, I was anxious to make an appointment. There was something about committing $250 toward a service that, you know, could totally be fake that terrified me, like when you order bogus beauty supplies off of Amazon. When it seems too good to be true, it almost always is. I finally clicked over to her website one morning when I should have been working and found her booked solid for four months. "She must be good

---

* Let it be known that basing a big life decision off of someone else's Instagram feed is a terrible way to go. Especially mine! Don't do anything I do. But definitely follow me on Instagram. Wait, maybe that's a terrible idea, too?

if she's this in demand!" I reasoned to myself. Either that, or there's just a butt-load of other weeping, grieving people out there missing their moms so desperately that they'll hand over hard-earned money to just about anyone. (I'm gonna go with a little of both.)

My session, which I booked in March, fell on the day after my birthday in mid-July. This was convenient, because when my husband looked at our Mint account listing our credit card charges and asked, "Hey, what's this thing for $250?" I shouted, "A BIRTHDAY PRESENT FOR MYSELF!" and ran to the bathroom before he could reply, "Wait, is this for that psychic?"

Now, this is obviously the wrong way to communicate in a marriage. But I'm only an expert in Dead Mom Grief, not relationships. Explaining to my husband that I was forking over a sweet chunk of our money to a psychic when we could be spending it at Costco on ten-pound bags of Parmesan cheese crackers and a sofa-sized package of guacamole was too much. (Yes, these items often top our Costco shopping list. What of it?)

I went into the day calm and relaxed, with zero expectations of what was to come. *Nope, wait, that's a lie.* I was a sweaty mess, with the sticky, relentless body moisture of a thoroughly chewed dog bone. That morning I rose with the dawn and prepped as if I were going on the first and only date of my life. I shaved my entire body, blow-dried and straightened my hair, and selected an outfit that screamed, "I WANT TO LOOK LIKE I DIDN'T PLAN THIS BUT OH YOU BETTER BELIEVE I PLANNED IT!" There were so many people I needed to impress: the psychic, my dead relatives, and the spirits of famous people who surely would want to stop in and say hi. (Look, I'm still pining for River Phoenix. A girl can dream.)

I tossed my children into the arms of their preschool teachers and raced back to my car, heading onto the freeway two hours before the appointment. Sure, LA traffic is a real thing, but I arrived at my appointment ninety minutes early. I took my time selecting the perfect parking spot and then spent the remaining eighty-seven minutes fidgeting in the driver's seat of my car, begging the spirit of my mom to show up. Finally, it was time. I peeled my leg skin away from the hot leather seat and began my trek to Psychic Town, USA.

Perhaps the strangest thing about the whole experience was how normal her office was. It looked like every temp agency I walked into in my twenties in New York City. The white-gray carpet matched the white-gray walls, which matched the white-gray cubicles, which matched my white-gray skin. There were no decorations; the place was sparse and dull, like every corporate office in America.

I checked in with the woman at the front desk, who pointed me toward a row of white-gray chairs. I plopped down, inhaling the familiar office smells of air-conditioning and microwaved Lean Cuisines. It only took a few minutes before the Psychic, in an outfit straight out of Banana Republic (the full-price stuff, not the sales rack), was standing in front of me, extending her hand.

"This way," she said pleasantly, summoning me toward a hallway brightly lit by the heavy summer sun pouring in through a wall of windows.

"I don't like to know anything about my clients," she explained, her voice gentle, as she opened the door to her office. "This way I don't have any thoughts or information flood my mind before our session."

I nodded in an attempt to be cool, as if I had previous experience with the psychic process. I glanced around, but her space was as nondescript as the rest of the building: a simple desk, comfortable chairs, an orchid miraculously alive in the corner. She waved me toward a chair, and I gingerly sat down and perched on the edge, clenching my butt cheeks together as if I were holding in gas.

"So," she said in a calm, even voice. "I invite all my clients to record our sessions so they can go back and listen to them."

"Okay," I said, as if I hadn't overcharged my iPhone and purchased a case with a battery pack for this very purpose. I laid it out on her desk, and she smiled at me. She was a human cup of Sleepytime tea, soothing and warm. There was nothing about her that reeked of scam artist; instead her vibe was that of a kind massage therapist who works on your knots for an hour and then comments on what great energy you have.

I hit record on my phone and immediately returned my gaze to her. She had already leaned back and shut her eyes. It was a minute before she spoke again.

I know what you are wondering, and so I am just going to tell you this first: no, she did not get *everything* right. Her reading was not 100 percent perfect; not every detail was correct or on point or exact. She brought up names that had no meaning to me,* which some might see as a red flag. And sure, it would be easy to write this all off as some sort of well-performed bullshit show. I've gone back and listened to our

---

* Victoria and Michael, if you are out there, the Psychic *really* wants me to know who you are!

session numerous times, and I can hear how I was so desper-
ate to say yes to everything she said, so much so that at times
I accepted those few inaccuracies, glossing over them because
I was so focused on believing.

But then, there were many things that she got so right, it
still makes my skin crawl when I play back the recording of
our session together. The details of my grandmother, her love
of nursing and education, the pull she felt between her passion
for her art and her family. My mother's cancer, how it left her
bloated and unable to eat. At one point, the Psychic laughed out
loud. "She's funny, your mom," she said with a genuine smile.
"She's telling me the cancer made her look like she was pregnant, and she's saying 'I never thought I'd do that again!'" This
was something *so* my mom that it left me startled and uneasy.
She captured the essence of her personality in a way that felt
eerie, as if she had been watching my mother her whole life.

And then there is this. Toward the end of our session she
paused and said, "You're also going to be writing about your
mother."

I let out an audible sob, like a whale trying to get another
whale's attention in the middle of the ocean. Undeterred, she
continued. "And she's going to help you with that and *is* helping you with that. But it feels almost more memoir than what
you've done in the past. It's very different, but it's great. She
loves it. She's so excited. She absolutely loves it. And I think
there's many funny stories about her, and there's a real joy you
can share with that."

Yes, dear reader, what you're wondering is correct: I was
in the middle of writing my book proposal at the time, the

book proposal for *this here book*. At that time I was not so much struggling with it as I was completely avoiding it, like a bad Tinder date who won't stop texting. Only a few people knew I was even working on it, and I never posted about it on social media. Sure, she could have Googled me and dug up my past work. But unless she hacked my computer or bugged my house, there's no way she had this information beforehand. She just *knew*.

"She's going to be sitting there with you," she continued. "But it feels unfinished. She enjoys looking at you and seeing the process. She's going to inspire you once you get into the flow of writing, and you will connect into the energy of her spirit. She's somebody that loves to make people laugh. She has good stories and funny stories, and she wants you to find the humor in it all."

Now, chances are you did not know my mother, but allow me to assure you: she did indeed love to make people laugh. This was a woman who, every time she caught me digging out a wedgie, would ask, "Are you going to the movies? Because you're picking your seat." She'd then cackle as I blushed, mortified that she'd got me yet again poking around up there. But even more so, my mom spent the nine months of her life with cancer finding the humor in *all* of it. She once joked that if she died before my wedding, I could have my flower girls sprinkle her ashes as they walked down the aisle. She made it okay to laugh at the terribleness of it all, and in doing this she made it bearable for the rest of us.

My dead grandfather showed up during the session to pressure me about my writing, too, because what family doesn't love a good old-fashioned pile on? Turns out, every dead family member of mine had been chilling on the Ikea couch in my office, sipping cans of sparkling water and watching me procrastinate by reading celebrity gossip blind items (90 percent of them are about Ben Affleck). And now it was time to let me know.

"He's talking about your written word," she said. "He's proud of you for that. But you haven't published a book yet. And you should. He wants you to do that. Get on with it, girl, is my feeling."

After each family member (and the few random strangers) blabbed, she offered up time for questions. We had only a few minutes left, and there was so much I could ask: Is God real? Had they met the cast of *Diff'rent Strokes*?

But all I could squeak out was this: "Am I an okay mother?"

My body shook as the words lingered. This was a question that haunted me. I was full of insecurities, about my career, my body, the fact that I claim I don't have time to volunteer but somehow have no problem finding hours to dedicate to *House Hunters International*. But above all, the thing I most wanted my mom to validate was that I was not screwing my kids up (too much). Because it was in motherhood that I longed for her the most, feeling her absence in every interaction with my daughters.

In hindsight it's kind of a dumb thing to ask, because what is the Psychic even going to say? "Hmmmm, yeah. About that. Actually your mom really wants you to know that you should cut back on the endless flow of Goldfish crackers you keep tossing in your kids' mouths. She's asking, 'Have you heard of fruit?' Also, your mom is telling me that she raised you to be a feminist and honestly, you're letting her down by allowing your daughters to watch *Lego Friends* on Netflix. It has no educational value and actually portrays women in kind of a questionable, sexist way."

Instead, her response was fairly anticlimactic. She nodded. "Yeah," she said. "You're doing a great job." I was slightly disappointed, hoping the spirits might give me specific feedback on the awesome parenting they'd observed. (I've cleaned vomit out of the cracks of car seats too many times for it to go unnoticed, thank you.) She paused and asked, "Do you see deer?"

Unlike most of America, Los Angeles is not flooded with herds of deer snarfing up every blade of grass in sight. In fact, I had only seen deer once in the four years I'd lived in Los Angeles, and it had just happened about four days before this meeting. I'd been driving with my family, winding through LA's vast and beautiful Griffith Park. We were on the main road, cruising right by the golf course, when my husband shouted, "Look, you guys! Deer!"

He slowed the car so we could watch them, because it was that rare of a sighting. There were two of them, just casually munching grass in the middle of the day as if it were no big thing. But it had been such an anomaly that we'd recounted the story to friends numerous times, despite the fact that "We saw deer!" is a pretty boring story to tell.

I recounted this sighting to the Psychic. "She sent you those," she said with a shrug, as if it were the most normal thing in the world.

We wrapped up, and I left the session buzzing. *My mom is with me!* my brain screamed. *And now she's going to hold my spiritual hand and help me write my book!* I couldn't believe my good fortune. Maybe, I thought to myself as I drove home, all those animal signs I'd grown disillusioned with were actually real. She *was* here with me and had been here all along. She was a beetle, a chipmunk, *and* a deer. Maybe she was every animal in the world!

But when I got home, my high crashed. I looked around my empty house, and suddenly the buzzing was gone, replaced by a deep, angsty sadness that held my stomach hostage. For a moment, the session had tricked me into feeling as if my mom were still alive. But nothing had actually changed. And now, sitting alone at my kitchen table, I felt furious. If my mom really was here, I wanted to talk to her every day. It was infuriating that some random woman could easily chat with her, while I had to wait in my yard hoping the random mourning dove taking a crap on my patio was also my mom. I was overcome with the urge to drive back to the Psychic's office and barricade myself in there for a week, just to discover what new adventures my mom and grandparents were getting into up in their Spirit Living Center. I had gotten a taste, and now I was thirsty for more receipts that my mom was, in fact, around me.

But the Psychic discourages clients from doing frequent visits ("every one to two years, if that"), suggesting instead that they begin to hone their own psychic ability to communicate with their dead people. This wasn't good enough for me. I wanted immediate results, and also I was lazy and didn't want to do the work to get them myself.

About six months after our session, I saw on Facebook that the Psychic was doing a live reading event. My entire outer layer of skin started tingling. I had come across it the morning of the show, and so I texted a few friends who I thought might enjoy watching a woman stand onstage and speak to the spirit ancestors of an audience made up of mostly middle-aged white women wearing way too much turquoise jewelry. Predictably, they were all busy. Not wanting to venture into the spirit party alone, I texted my reliably cynical and dear friend, Susannah.

"Can I convince you to go see my psychic do live readings tonight?" I pled. Her response came quick. "I think psychics are scam artists who prey on the bereaved," read her text. "So no."

I didn't even bother asking my husband, who had very quietly narrowed his eyes at me when I'd announced my first psychic visit. So I did what any reasonable woman in her midthirties would do on a Friday night: I went to the psychic reading event alone.

The crowd gathered in the theater lobby was way more diverse than I expected. Yes, the gangs of older women with frosty blond hair, bejeweled flip-flops, and flowy Chico's pants were there, clutching their tickets in hands heavy with giant silver rings. But the rest of the crowd was an unpredictable mix, like an Al-Anon meeting. A cool skater guy who looked like Puck from *The Real World: San Francisco* (best season ever— I dare you to debate me on this) chatted with another handsome skater guy I would have totally tried to date in 2001. Families wandered to their seats with kids and babies in tow. Next to me, a balding man with a light brown beard tapped away on a flip phone and made eyes with a woman seated halfway across the auditorium. Was it his wife? Was he here to pick up grieving widows? I got no cell service, so instead I made up his life story in my head to entertain myself as we waited.

Finally, the Psychic arrived. The second she opened her mouth she was warm and light, instantly comforting. You got why dead people are desperate to chill with her.

"This person who comes to me died of cancer," she said, standing directly in front of my section of the audience. Immediately my bones perked up inside my body, bouncing against my skin. "Pancreatic cancer," she continued.

Oh my God. My entire body flushed with nervous excitement. *It's happening again!* My spirit was the *best* spirit! My mom was back to catch me up on what's new in her life (still dead and loving it, I assumed) and to send me more glowing messages from beyond!

"It's an older man," she continued. *No. No no no no.* My brain raced as my stomach dropped in disappointment. Her words felt like an insult, spiting me, mocking me for coming. I looked around, bewildered, certain she was about to correct herself. As I did, I noticed three other women in the crowd perk up. *Oh.*

All of us were there because the same piece-of-garbage cancer had destroyed our lives, taking someone from us whom we loved so deeply that we each paid $35 to sit in a room and try to talk to their ghosts. The sad realization sunk my shoulders, and I slid low in my seat.

I watched as a woman a few rows in front of me wept as the Psychic spoke to her dad, a jovial, larger-than-life man who suffered the same fate as my mom. We clapped as she finished the reading, some audience members in tears, moved by the sheer emotion of it all.

At the start of every reading that followed, you could feel the entire room hold their breath in anticipation, wishful that this time would be their turn. Over the next two hours the Psychic connected with the spirits of a drug dealer whose gun death remained unsolved, a Holocaust survivor, an old grandmother who sang opera, a son who died too young, a man who overdosed, another who took his own life, and a tall dad who always carried coins in his pockets.

But my mom never came.

By the end of the two-and-a-half-hour event, the divide between those chosen and those not felt sharp and clear. The chosen ones were the celebrities of the room: golden, superior, possessing a knowledge the rest of us common folk would never have. They sparkled with the shine of being picked, leaving the rest of us to wonder: *Why didn't our dead people show up? Why do they hate us?* Not having my mom appear left me crushed and hurt, wondering what I did wrong. Because let's be real—nothing feels worse than being ghosted by an actual ghost.

I left the event and drove home, saddled with the same wired, hollow feeling I had after my initial reading. I pulled into my driveway but stayed in my car, soaking up the quiet and the darkness, exhausted. Not just by the night, but by the chasing, the hunt, the years-long desire to tamp down my grief with some sort of assurance that my mom is still here.

You don't need to experience death to know that there's no such thing as closure; anyone who's been dumped or burned by an unrequited love can tell you that. Nothing about losing my mom has ever felt open and shut; the only thing that's absolute is that she's dead. I have tried to find bits and pieces of her in every crack and surface of the earth, in every moment. Almost every day I look up to the sky and think, *Are you here? Are you seeing this?*

She is nowhere, but she is everywhere, too. And so I keep looking for her, and beyond her, too. Because after all, the

Psychic said, "She wants you to find the humor in it all." And maybe she wasn't referring to this book at all.

Maybe she was simply talking about life.

———

THINGS TO CONSIDER BEFORE SEEING A PSYCHIC

WOULD YOU RATHER SPEND THAT MONEY ON A REALLY NICE PAIR OF JEANS?

A good psychic medium is most likely going to be expensive. It's easy to get caught up in the excitement of visiting someone who might be able to connect you to your dead mom, but take a deep breath and evaluate if it's where you want to burn your cash. Because seriously—jeans are also a great investment. And if you decide to go the shopping route, you can always try to see a good medium at a live, ticketed event, which will likely be way cheaper than a one-on-one visit.

ARE YOU EMOTIONALLY STABLE ENOUGH TO HANDLE IT?

My experience "talking" to my mother through a psychic medium was way more emotionally exhausting than I expected. I assumed it would offer closure, like one final conversation with an ex. Now for some people, I'm sure this is exactly what they get out of the experience. But for me it was unsettling, setting off a lot of intense emotions and new waves of grief. I liked it, but it wasn't a walk in the park. (It was more like a walk in the cemetery. LOL?) So if you're not in a great place emotionally, give yourself a pass.

PREPARE TO BE TEASED. LIKE, A LOT.

People think I'm bananas for spending my money on psychics and have no problem telling me so.

IT MAY BE A TOTAL BUST.

I saw one psychic medium two times. The first was magical; it was as if she exposed this entire spiritual world right under my nose. The second time was like one big fart noise: pfffffffft. Nothing really happened, and she didn't tell me any new, exciting information. If you go into it with zero expectations, you can't be disappointed.

DO YOU LIKE DISCUSSING CELEBRITY MEDIUMS?

I sure hope so, because the second you tell someone you've seen a psychic medium, you'll spend the rest of the night listening to their opinion on John Edward, the Long Island Medium, and the Hollywood Medium. You will have this conversation for the rest of your life. Only you can decide if it's worth it.

13

The One Who Never Calls

This chapter is about my ex-boyfriend.

I am telling you this in case you are my ex-boyfriend, in which case: *Hey! How are you? I'm so honored that you're reading my book. I stalked your wedding on Instagram, and it looked beautiful. Please accept my belated congratulations. Also, this next chapter is about you, so feel free to skip it. Or not. Either way, thanks for the memories, and I'm sorry you decided to date a writer.*

My ex-boyfriend, who for the sake of his anonymity will be known in this chapter as Matt Damon, and I dated for three and a half years. He was handsome and odd, a perpetually stoned artist who skateboarded around the ivy-covered brick buildings that made up our college campus and whipped out his sketchbook when he didn't feel like talking to people, which was often. He had a closed-off, curmudgeonly quality to him—he once told me early on in our relationship that he wasn't sure if he "felt emotions." But he was also extraordinarily curious and bright, a fearless explorer of the world, and a person who could give you shit but also take it. He was naturally athletic and a member of our college ski team, so most importantly, he had a nice butt.

I started crushing on Matt Damon toward the end of our freshman year. I had just gotten out of a relationship with my high school boyfriend, Ben Affleck, who dumped me the weekend before Valentine's Day at a sandwich shop. He had driven all the way up to Maine from Massachusetts to watch me in my first acting role as "Mom" in an educational play for kids about molestation titled *No More Secrets*. He sat through a performance in the small black-box theater on campus, with an audience of just four adults—the director, my parents, and him. I sang my heart out in the finale—"No more secrets, starting today!" After hugging my mom and dad good-bye he took me out for turkey subs and broke the news: it was over. He still loved me, he said, but "like one of my guy friends." Just what every gal wants to hear! I responded by storming out of the restaurant and, once outside, throwing my coffee at him. But it got sucked up by the icy Maine wind, and the lid popped off, and it splattered all over my head. I have *no* idea why he dumped a catch like me.

There I was, eighteen, single, with a closet full of terrible boot-cut corduroys and hardly any self-esteem or dating experience. As the fog of my first heartbreak lifted, I started eyeing Matt Damon in his giant hoodies and skater sneakers. I became quickly smitten but was certain he'd never be interested. I was a too tall, freshly dumped, inexperienced hippie weirdo in a sea of toned girls with names like Shelby and

Paige, who looked like they just bushwhacked their way out of a J.Crew catalog with their lacrosse sticks.

But that summer I worked at a dog biscuit bakery in Burlington, Vermont, got a tattoo of a butterfly right above my butt crack, and made out with a long-haired Deadhead named Shane, who drove a two-door sports car with a vanity plate that read "StrItUp."* I returned to college as a slightly more confident sophomore who was slowly growing into the giant eyebrow ring that hung off my face. My social circle overlapped with Matt Damon's, and soon we were flirting with each other the way only college kids in the '90s could: I took black-and-white pictures of him skateboarding for my photography class, and a few weeks later he asked if I could drive him forty-five minutes to the Portland airport to pick up a friend visiting from out of town. It was our first date.

We fell in that kind of intense college love that leads you to willingly sleep in a twin bed with another person. I loved that Matt Damon was broody, good-looking, and unassumingly hip. He had an edge that was missing from most of the guys at our small, preppy college, and he didn't care that I wasn't traditionally girly, athletic, or cool. He played me obscure Oakland hip-hop, and I dragged him to Phish shows. When we studied abroad, he in Nepal and me in South Africa, we packed voice recorders in our bags so we could send each other audiotapes in addition to letters. Our friend circle was the same, so much so that my roommates never minded that he was

---

* For my readers who somehow escaped reggae in college, this is a Bob Marley reference. Sigh.

always around. And we spent time with each other's families: he gamely attended dinners with my parents and stored his clothes and CD collection in their garage. I clogged the only toilet at his stepmom's house, which he then plunged for me without complaint. It was true love.

After our senior year, when I moved to New York, he helped pack a U-Haul with my stuff. He endured the slow, CD-player-less ride to Brooklyn, and then hung around for a few days before taking off for Europe, where he had planned to live until the following summer. We probably should have taken this geographical split as a sign that we were done. Instead we barreled on back into a long-distance relationship, determined and teeth-gritted. Our relationship had become its own living, breathing entity that stretched through cities and people, existing way beyond the two of us.

This is what made it so hard to finally admit we were done. Because despite our devotion and connection, underlying issues flared up throughout our three and a half years together. The main one being: Matt Damon and I were *totally* wrong for each other. I was incredibly sensitive and empathetic and craved emotional connection; he was cool, distant, and independent. He ripped bong hits on the regular to release stress, and I was so tightly wound and anxious that being stoned made me a paranoid mess. I was an extrovert; he was a person-who-left-parties-without-saying-good-bye-trovert.

Ultimately, figuring this out about your relationship is a good thing. This is, after all, the beauty of college relationships—you learn about the kind of person you don't want to end up with in the long run. But during our time as a couple, I wrapped myself up in our relationship like a security blanket. My own insecurities left me terrified that if we ended things, he'd move on with an army of hot women, and I'd never find someone who could love me or even be attracted to me again. (Remember when I mentioned my low self-esteem? Yeah, I wasn't kidding.) It took leaving our college bubble and moving to New York City for me to realize that the world was full of humans who might actually find me attractive. Who cares if I was even into them—men (and women) wanted to bone me!

This awakening left me spinning. Also I was horny and hadn't seen Matt Damon in months. It was 2002, and internet cafés were still acceptable hang-out spots. Staying in touch was a challenge, and the distance—and my lust for the aforementioned New Yorkers eager to suck my face—eventually made it clear that we were dunzo. So on the day before yet another Valentine's Day, I bought a ten-dollar calling card and a six pack of Miller Lite at the bodega down the street and unceremoniously chugged a beer and then called him up and ended things. It was anticlimactic, a long time coming, and ultimately a relief. Sure, I spent the first week holding back tears at work, my eyes swollen like two overly ripe peaches. But my sadness about the breakup was also tinged with regret and shame that I had not been confident enough to end things earlier, because our incompatibility had been clear to me even at the beginning. (But never you worry—that's what therapy in your thirties is for!) A month after our breakup I was making out on a bamboo mat with a stand-up comic from my Improv 101 class who slept in an empty room because he was too broke to afford furniture. Things were really coming up Kate!

When Matt Damon returned to America that summer, he invited me out to dinner. I was eager to go, for three reasons:

1. I still cared for him a great deal and was excited to see him!
2. Let's be real: I wanted to show off the new, thinner, shorter-haired, H&M-shopping, New York version of myself. My entire exterior had become one big post-college humblebrag.
3. The biggest reason of all: A few weeks prior I had heard through the friend grapevine that he was now dating our mutual college friend, Minnie Driver, and the news that they might be together stabbed at me like a nurse trying and failing to find a vein for an IV.

There we were again, face-to-face, shoved into a two-person table at a restaurant where all the two-person tables were uncomfortably close together. It was genuinely wonderful to see him, because despite all our differences and my own hesitations about our relationship, here was a human who knew me and my life better than almost anyone else. We chatted for a few minutes, my heart racing, and he presented me with a bracelet he had purchased for me during his travels. It was delicate and silver, and I immediately loved it, the kind of timeless piece of jewelry that holds up no matter the changing fashion trends of the time. It was also an incredibly kind gesture, an act of true affection from a person who clearly still cared about me despite us no longer being together. Matt Damon had not been right for me, nor had he been a perfect partner, but he was an inherently good person.

The entire interaction filled me with immense joy. *See, world!* I thought to myself smugly. *Amicable breakups are possible. Some of us are capable of rising above!*

And then I asked him if he was dating our friend.

"Yes," he said, his face gentle. "It just kind of happened. I'm going to move in with her in—"

I did not let Matt Damon finish his sentence. A rage volcano erupted in me so fiercely that I vomited angry word lava all over the table. It was a mixture of "How could you?" and "How could she?" and "I don't want your fucking pity bracelet" and then back to "How could you?"

And the answer is very simple: he could because . . . he could. We weren't together. Matt Damon and Minnie Driver both had free will and the right to pursue love. There was absolutely nothing wrong with them being together.

And yet.

Anyone who has done the dumping in a relationship knows that these furious, horrible, angry feelings betray all rational thought. There is no way to coherently explain the fire you feel when the person you dumped finds love before you— and with a mutual friend, no less! These are irrational feelings; they are not rooted in logic, and above all, they're unfair. Your ex can date whomever they damn well please. Theoretically we all know this and get it. But no logic or reason can stop this particular kind of demon rage. Once this jealous beast is implanted in your gut, you unleash it like projectile vomit after a night of binge drinking. It's hot and putrid, and nothing you do can stop it from pouring out of you.

Because the simple truth of it was: I was embarrassed that he had moved on and also that I was so crushed by it. That kind of anger is humiliating: it reveals all your gnawing insecurities to people whom you desperately want to imagine you as totally together. Instead, everyone saw what a hot, angry, insecure mess I was. And the first person to witness it was Matt Damon himself. After hearing the news and letting all my hurt feelings come rumbling out of my mouth, I ran out of yet another restaurant in a heartbroken fury, storming out onto some East Village avenue. It was pouring rain—sometimes life is an incredibly accurate cliché. Matt Damon followed me, trying to calm me down with a hug. I flung the bracelet at him, screamed some more awful things, and hurled my dripping body into a yellow cab that miraculously happened to be lurking nearby.

We avoided each other for almost two years.

But when his relationship with Minnie Driver finally ended, he reached out, and our friendship was reborn in earnest. What followed was an easy friendship, in which we joked over email and on the phone, spilling about dating and new relationships. Our conversations were filled with details about the ups and downs of our individual paths—me performing comedy and seriously dating a new boyfriend, him single and applying to art school. We occasionally hung out in New York, and when our five-year college reunion came around in June 2006, we funneled beer together like old friends. I laughed watching him mack on the single women we'd graduated with years ago. Our relationship finally felt normal and in a better place than when we were dating.

And then a few weeks later, my mom's cancer diagnosis sliced my life up into a million nightmarish little pieces. Matt Damon sent sympathetic emails, checking in on me from time to time, and voiced his support. We even talked over email a few weeks before she died, and on the day she passed he was on the short list of "important people" I asked my best friend to contact with the news, which she did.

And then I never heard from him again.

In the weeks that followed my mom's death, a gajillion other people reached out to me. I received flowers, handwritten letters, emails, texts, donations in my mom's name. The response was overwhelming, and I still worry—to this day—that I've never properly expressed the gratitude I feel for the support I received from strangers, close friends, and everyone in between. Human beings from all corners of my life stumbled out of the woodwork to show me kindness when I needed it the most, and it carried me through the worst time in my life.

Except Matt Damon. He did not call, or email, or text, or send a card. And the more support I received, the more his absence became a gaping wound hemorrhaging all over my insides. I was devastated that this person, who had shared my life and known my mother and family, was choosing not to reach out in the moment that mattered most. And the anger I felt (yoinks, see a pattern?) seemed so gross and ungrateful when the rest of the world stepped up so fiercely to support me. I was ashamed at how mad I was at him. Why was I consumed by one person's silence when every other spot in my life shone with love?

(The answer is that I am a flawed, imperfect human. Duh.)

A few weeks after my mom died, I asked my best friend where da hell Matt Damon was. "Why hasn't he written me?" I asked over G-chat. "Should I write him? Or is it not a big deal? I thought I would hear from him by now."

She replied thoughtfully, because she is the best person I know. "I think he doesn't know what to say," she typed. "As you

know, he's not so good at this stuff. It's a big deal if it's important to you. He's definitely thinking about you, I just think he
doesn't know what to do."

But I didn't reach out to him. One, because I am a coward
who is so scared of confrontation that I have never complained
to my neighbor about them letting their dog bark outside at
five in the morning for two straight years. But also because
I was sad, and tired, and deeply depressed, and I just simply
wanted him to do it on his own.

And so I waited. And waited. I waited over two years.
During this time many wonderful things happened: I got a
job I loved desperately; I married a fantastic person; I found
relief in yoga and therapy. Anthony and I moved to Brooklyn
and finally found an apartment with a dishwasher. I made the
transition to skinny jeans. My life was on fire, despite the grief
abyss that sucked me in on the regular. But Matt Damon's
inability to reach out chewed me up like mosquitos on a summer night. Two years deep into letting his silence devastate me,
I finally unloaded it all on my therapist. She listened patiently
as my words came up in chunks, broken up by heaving sobs.
When I was done, she thought for a moment and then said, "It
sounds to me like you're protecting your mother. You're hurt on
her behalf because you feel like him not responding is disre-
specting her, too."

And boy, did that make sense. I wasn't just hurt by his
absence; I was hungry for justice for my dead mom. I simply
wanted him to acknowledge that she had mattered. *This* is
what heated an anger so deep inside me that I had countless
nightmares in which I confronted him about it. *This* fueled
the emails to my friends typed with fingers so furious the *F*

key on my laptop stopped working. I was like Inigo Montoya in *The Princess Bride*, existing only to avenge my dead mother's honor. Matt Damon was my six-fingered man.

And then, one day, out of the blue I heard from him. He sent me a friend request on Facebook.

Of all the ways to reach out after two and a half years of silence, he picked Facebook. *FACEBOOK*. And let me tell you, when you've stewed for two years over someone not contacting you after your beloved mother's death, there's nothing quite as gut-punchingly poetic as their name popping up in your Facebook notifications.

And there was a message, too.

It was generally pleasant and casual, filling me in on his girlfriend and career plans and casually asking if I was excited a mutual friend was moving to New York. But it also included a masterful backhanded compliment, in which he simultaneously complimented my career as a pop culture talking head while also probably kinda insinuating that it was trashy. In hindsight, I can see he intended it as a genuinely kind observation. But I was looking to find every reason to be furious with him, so it was the icing on my rage cake. And now I was ready to eat the entire thing with my hands.

I had literally dreamed of confronting Matt Damon about his silence for years, and now here he was, all one hundred and fifty words of him, in my inbox. I had thought for so long that finally hearing from him would make me feel better. But I was almost ill looking at his message. Instead of assuaging my anger, his message threw kindling on it, turning it from a small campfire into a rapidly spreading wildfire. His tone was so casual and friendly that it was clear to me that he had no idea he'd broken one of society's most basic of rules: reach out to someone after they lose a loved one, ya dumb fuck. (I added that last part in, but otherwise this *is* what society says.) But it was that he did it over Facebook that really made me fume. Facebook, where one can literally fart out status updates. Facebook, where people post 9/11 conspiracy memes and slow-cooker chili recipes. Facebook, where I once trolled West Elm for a week after they failed to deliver a dresser I ordered. *Facebook.*

This is not to say that Mark Zuckerberg's social media baby is void of value. In fact, when it comes to grieving, it's a great place to update people on a loved one, to send messages of support, to find people to connect with when you're isolated and alone. And yes, it *is* a great place to share slow-cooker chili recipes. (9/11 conspiracy memes, not so much.) But his message contained not one mention of my mother or any condolences, which would've been seriously belated yet much appreciated anyway. So his words felt particularly hollow, meaningless, and all the more lazy when they showed up with a "bing!" in my Facebook inbox. I pounded out my reply on my keyboard so hard it was as if I were trying to jam the keys so that they never worked again. My reply was cutting! It was pointed! It was civil but icy! I bragged about my accomplishments—my marriage, my yoga teacher training, the television career he had kinda dissed—and I topped it off with the polite sugges-tion that we never talk again. I proudly examined my word venom. Then I hit send.

His reply was swift; it landed in my inbox in less than an hour. He clarified his comment about my TV appearance, which was, he explained, intended to be a compliment. And then he said, in plain terms, that it simply never dawned on him to reach out to me after my mom died—not for any malicious reason, but because he didn't think he would be someone I'd want to talk to about my loss. So he stayed silent, but assured me that he had mourned my mom, too. Crying about it, even! Most of all he seemed shocked and hurt by my words, and sad that I wanted to sever all ties.

I wrote back again, this time with a cooler head. I detailed the outpouring of support I received, so that the lack of any sort of communication from him only stood out against it. And I said that it had made me reflect on the kind of people and relationships I wanted in my life, and this was not it. His response was short and apologetic. He explained once again that he was not conscious of the fact that he never reached out after she died, and that he'd try and do that for people in the future. He then unfriended me on Facebook, as I asked, and we never messaged each other again. (Though we did have one final interaction at a friend's wedding a few months later. I was nervous. It was cordial. The end.)

There is an Ani DiFranco lyric that says, "Maybe we are both good people who have done some bad things." (I just crossed the Quote Ani DiFranco in Your Memoir line; I am so very sorry.) Every time I remember how my relationship with Matt Damon unraveled, both as a couple and later as friends, I think of a million ways I could have done it all better. There's an anger stage in grieving, though I think all stages of grieving play out in a parallel plane rather than in succession. My anger happened alongside my sadness and my denial. And it was all knotted together: a rubber-band ball of uncomfortable feelings. Maybe it was easier for me to be mad at Matt

Damon's silence than it was to dig into the thing that truly made me mad: my mom not being here. Or maybe I was simply destroyed by the fact that someone I cared about failed to acknowledge this simple fact. Or maybe it's both, because grief is layered and complex and a Rubik's Cube of emotions.

"I don't think you can assume that someone's silence means that they don't care," my dad, in editor mode, said to me the first time he read a draft of this chapter. "Yeah, but . . . " I tried, but didn't come up with much of a reply. I gave up, because in truth, his words sent my brain churning in a new direction. I'd spent years assuming that Matt Damon's silence meant he didn't care about my mom or recognize the earth-shattering grief I was battling. Maybe he did; he just didn't know how to express it or how much it would have meant for me to hear it from him. But even if my dad is right, which he probably is because he's my dad, it will never move me beyond this fact: Matt Damon should have reached out.

One of the challenges of grieving is coming to terms with the fact that not everyone is going to do it exactly how you want. The world will go on in ways that offend you; friends will say the wrong thing, or worse—nothing at all. Perhaps it's not because they don't know what to say, but because they don't know how to say it. Maybe they're afraid that when they do say something, it's going to come out all weird or make your grief worse. And I get this. But I also know how much it can mean when you're living in a nightmare to receive even just a couple of sentences of support. If you ever find yourself in Matt Damon's shoes, I say this: just try. It is better to attempt communication than to do nothing at all. And hey, if you find yourself without words, use these: "How do you like them apples?"

Wait, no, I'm sorry, that's a line from Matt Damon's Oscar-winning film, *Good Will Hunting*. What I mean is, try this: "Jason Bourne is dead, you hear me?"

Goddamn it, also wrong.

You know what? There isn't a *right* thing to say. Just say *something*. That is, quite simply, good enough.

SAMPLE DEAD MOM SYMPATHY CARDS WHICH YOU MAY PLAGIARIZE TO YOUR HEART'S CONTENT

FOR AN ACQUAINTANCE:

Dear [insert name here],
I am so very sorry to hear about the loss of your mom.
You have my deepest sympathy during this hard time.
Sending all my love to you and your family.
Sincerely,
Your Name

WHEN YOU DON'T KNOW YOUR FRIEND'S DEAD MOM:

Dear [insert name here],
I am so very sorry to hear about the loss of your mom.
Even though I did not know her personally, I know—
based on how great you are—that she must have been
an incredible person. [And if you did know her, just say

"She was truly an incredible person." And if this is not true, just say nothing at all.] You have my deepest sympathy during this time. I love you and am here for you.
Sincerely,
Your Name

WHEN YOU'RE REACHING OUT TO SOMEONE WITH WHOM YOU'RE ON, ER, LESS THAN GOOD TERMS:
Dear [insert name here],
I am so very sorry to hear about the loss of your mom. Even though we have not spoken in a while, you are always in my heart, and you and your family have my deepest sympathy during this hard time.
Sincerely,
Your Name

14

DeadMom.com

M y friendship with Matt Damon crashed and burned on Facebook Messenger, but that didn't stop me from embracing the internet as my own personal grieving station. Because if there's one thing my grief loves, it's attention. Chalk it up to my own social media addiction or one of the many personality disorders I certainly must have. But it never fails: when I am sad about my mom, and in that dark, hollow place where it feels as if no one will ever understand how I could still possibly be so devastated even though she's been dead forever, I go online to seek solace, commiseration, and support, and to read about Lindsay Lohan promoting her new Greek nightclub* while speaking in a British accent.

I have cherished the internet like a dear friend since the moment I held an America Online disc in my teenage hand. The sound of the modem logging into my computer— like the noises an AI robot would make while being murdered—still sends my heart soaring. It's that feeling I had as

---

* This is real, it's called Lohan, and it's in Athens—meet you there?

a sixteen-year-old that still lights up in me—of being oh-so-close to a community of people who get me. Back in 1996 I was an awkward hippie just trying to find my people, and AOL had an entire chat room dedicated to Phish fans. This is where I sat, for hours each night, discussing set lists and writing terrifyingly bad poetry about my teenage depression, which was always met with supportive words.

This is how it has been for my life since then: the internet is home (it even became my job). So it was no shock that one night, just days after learning about my mom's diagnosis, I set up a blog solely dedicated to her illness and my attempt to train for a half marathon and raise money for pancreatic cancer research. I titled it "RunningForMyMom," because my creative juices were clearly not flowing that night and also, simply, this is what I was trying to do.

"My sassy, awesome, and beautiful mom Martha, age 55, was diagnosed with Pancreatic Cancer on June 14, 2006," I wrote in my first post. "Her diagnosis is Stage IV with metastases on the liver, which roughly translates into 'THIS SUCKS BIG TIME.'"

I ran for my mom—twice, in fact—and raised over $20,000, which I donated to Massachusetts General Hospital. This was my desperate attempt to have some control over her cancer, and it helped a little. (Plus going on outdoor runs is a great place to sob openly where no one can see you! Highly recommend. 10/10 stars.) Friends and strangers cheered me on in the comments, and every donation to my cause felt like a hug. My local newspaper even wrote up a front-page story on my fundraising effort, featuring a smiling photo of my mom and me.

But something about crafting the experience into a story online felt misleading; I was portraying my mom's illness as manageable, only showing people the parts that were easy to digest. My tone was almost always optimistic, and the me I presented online was tough and gritty, as if I were surviving my sadness simply by lacing up my shoes and jogging it out. But the person typing those words was in deep despair, panicked, clawing at a world that was unraveling as my mom slipped further and further away.

Most of the site is gone now, lost when I moved the blog over to a dedicated URL, which I let die soon after my mom did. I didn't have it in me anymore to keep it up, to run for anyone or anything. I left the site when she left me, too lost to put anything else back into it.

In the months that followed her death, the sadness came flying out of my fingertips. It was often way too hard to move my mouth to say actual words about it. Instead I shut down when humans asked me how I was doing, eking out a smile and a high-pitched "I'm okay!" But when I was home and slumped in front of the TV with my laptop roasting on my thighs, I quickly turned to my favorite confidante: the internet. I found solace blogging on Tumblr, dumping my emotions into raw, rambling posts that would often result in a friend texting me, "I saw yr post abt yr mom, r u doing ok?" It was a relief to put those emotions somewhere, and placing them on the web validated them in the exact way that I needed. In those moments after, as I watched the likes, faves, and reblogs tick up and up and up, my grief was alleviated. The gratification was instant, but then quickly over. The second the emotions spilled out,

I filled right back up with new ones—prickly, awful feelings that left me raw and beaten down.

It's been over ten years, and I'm *still* posting about my mom online. You'd think I'd have learned by now that the internet moves on, even when you do not. Instead I keep chasing that feeling, memorializing her online to try to keep her alive. And the experience is the same every time: once the last person likes the post, and the reminders stop lighting up my phone, it's over. The satisfaction I get from forcing others to remember her disappears when I realize that they've already forgotten her again. They move on to something else, while I'm still stuck, unable to peel myself away from my grief.

Crafting these online remembrances never actually accomplishes what I so desperately want them to. Six hundred and eight likes on an Instagram photo of my mother with her bad perm and that one red sweater with the shoulder pads can't suddenly bring her back to life, breathing on the other end of my phone line, calling to remind me to buy my train tickets home for Christmas. It does not blot up the pain I still feel staining my wonderful, joyous life. You cannot fill a void up with faves and likes. Posting about my grief is like eating In-N-Out after a really long day. It's satisfying in the moment, but in the end it doesn't actually make me feel any better. I'm left feeling full but hollow, and with a gross taste in my mouth.

But this hasn't stopped me from sharing all my sads, though it's less frequent these days. Still, on her birthday in November, or the anniversary of her death every March, I set up a digital memorial in her honor. I've done long, rambling blog posts about the life-and-death elements in her favorite song ("Layla" by Eric Clapton—the electric version, thank you very much) and a photo of birds soaring through the sky. Lately it's been Instagram posts featuring old photos of her in saucer-like glasses with a middle part, holding lil' baby me, or a short but sentimental, weepy status update. "Today is the anniversary of my mom's death," I write. "She would be 65 years old now."

Occasionally I ask people to remember her for a moment, to say her name out loud. The likes pile up; her best friends and my aunts chime in with their stories and memories. "There isn't a day that goes by where we don't think of her," they say. And I know it's true, but something about reminding the world, about typing it out and tacking it up on a virtual wall, makes it concrete. It says: She was here. She's still here. Even if you forget tomorrow, at least you remember now.

There are times when I worry if I am treading into "too much" territory, nervous someone might start to think less of me the more I publish my darkest, scariest feelings. Before my own mom died, I would have lovingly side-eyed someone for hammering out sensitive, weepy Dead Mom Tributes online. Even now, crafting these posts at times feels trite and embarrassing, like I'm admitting a weakness I should have conquered or, at least, done a better job at covering up. Every time I take to my computer to type out my pain, there's always that husky voice (the voice in my head is very sexy, okay?) that whispers, "You should be over this by now, Kate."

I assume this panic is a direct result of my Puritan roots; in New England your ability to swallow your pain and shake it off is as coveted as Red Sox season tickets. Because even though I declare the voice in my head to be utter bullshit, I still let it sting me in my more insecure moments.

Because the truth is, I'm not over it. I'm never going to be over it. The endless blog posts and Instagram pictures, late-night tweets and Facebook updates aren't just about getting my pain out or remembering her. I don't just want to be seen; I want my grief to be seen, too. I want her to last, her fire to keep burning even though cancer snuffed it out. I want people to know how much it hurts. I want people to feel how *bad* it is. It's an attempt to give a body to the enormous swell of pain inside. But no post or photo will ever capture it. It is beyond social media, beyond words or photos or sad song lyrics. Those things are useless when it comes to truly capturing my grief. It's like showing someone who's never seen water a dripping faucet and then trying to explain what standing in a rainstorm feels like.

Even though she was never on social media, I feel her absence there. My fingers itch to follow her, if only I could. My mom was an internet whiz; she have would figured out Twitter and Instagram, downloaded every app onto her phone and made her accounts private, and then called me to go online and check to make sure her accounts *were* actually private. She would follow Kim Kardashian on Snapchat, text me updates about her drama with Taylor Swift, and then send me pictures of herself using all the stupid filters with my dad lurking in the background. My mom would have had the internet presence of a voracious tween.

Just knowing how she would have loved being a stereotypical middle-aged mom on Facebook gives me pangs of longing, simply because she's missing out. On her most recent birthday, I uploaded a short video of my two daughters singing her

"Happy Birthday." The moment happened so organically that I barely caught any of it on camera—one minute I was casually mentioning to them that that day was her birthday, and the next second they were belting out, "Happy bird-day, dear Marfa," like they knew her. The likes on the video rolled in as they always do, and my mom's college roommate wrote, "Oh, your mom would have LOVED that so very much." And in that one comment lives all my sadness: it's not just what she's missing online that hurts. It's that she's missing *all* of it. And oh, how she would have loved it all so much. This is the hurt that keeps me at my keyboard, even after all these years, trying to make people understand this throbbing, endless ache that I'll never be able to really describe at all.

DEAD MOM BLOG POST MAD LIBS

Just fill in the blanks to get yourself the perfect piece of sentimental online writing.

Black-and-white photo of [noun] looking [adjective].

Today is my mom's [important date]. This day is [adjective] for me for many reasons, and I can't stop [verb]. I keep thinking of my mom, and how she was always [verb] in [place]. When I was a kid, my mom would always tell me [piece of advice]. She'd look at me [adverb], with her [adjective] [color] eyes, and I knew everything was going to be [adjective]. Now, I know she's in [place], feeling so [adjective] of me. Thinking of her like this is the only way I can [verb] at night. I [emotional verb] you so much, Mom.

15

—·ᡣ᠊ᢶ᠊Ɑᢗᡢᢶᢣᡧ·—

I Learned It from Watching You

The story my mom always told went like this: I was born in the midst of my parents planning a cross-country move from Boston to San Francisco. Weeks after my birth, my dad headed out to the West Coast to find an apartment. My mom and grandmother followed later with me, a six-week-old fat-faced baby who looked like a tiny old Italian man with a Jake Gyllenhaal head of dark hair, in tow. When we arrived at our two-bedroom Marina apartment (my poor-ass parents paved the way for so many future Facebook employees), my grandmother set up her own bedroom in a closet. She shoved one end of a tiny blow-up mattress into the closet and created her own little private living space.

This story was repeated over the years, always to highlight my sweet, selfless, no-drama grandmother's ingenious ways of blending in and making herself invisible. But when my mom died, it quickly took on a new meaning for me: I would never have my mom to help me navigate parenting. She would never get to shove her own crappy mattress into a closet in my apartment. I would have to go at it alone.

This loss becomes pointedly clear the second you get knocked up. Suddenly the world is filled with grandmas-to-be planning baby showers, knitting baby sweaters, sharing family heirlooms, and planning chunks of time to move in with their kids to help care for the baby once it arrives. After my daughter arrived, every woman I met at my breastfeeding group or mommy-and-me yoga had a story of their mother moving in with them when the baby came, cooking obscene amounts of food, doing laundry shifts at all hours of the night, and generally making things just a little bit easier for everyone. Plus, their moms had been through it before, so they were permanently on-call 24/7 to ask about all aspects of parenting—weird poops, diaper rashes, sore nipples, sleep schedules. And there I was, left to cull through my memories of my mother like an old prospector digging for gold, only I was extracting bits and pieces of parenting advice she'd espoused over the years.

I retained only two things. First, she very proudly gave birth to my brother and me without any medication. "Just ice chips!" she'd chirp, not even trying to hide her bragging. Both our baby albums contain very graphic pictures of our mom laid out on hospital beds, bloody and with full '70s pubic hair on display. She was not ashamed of her body or what she did to bring us into the world. She loved breastfeeding, to the point where, were she alive today, she'd probably identify as a "lactivist."

The other thing I remembered is that we'd cheer for the ob-gyn who delivered me as he ran the Boston Marathon every year. "There's the doctor who delivered you!" my mom would shout, clapping, as a herd of runners passed by.

I was twenty-seven when my mom died; I had barely even thought about getting married then, much less having kids. It never dawned on me to ask about her experiences moving across the country with an infant, breastfeeding babies, or surviving life with a toddler and a newborn at home.

Once, after she died, her childhood friend told me how she'd been present the time my mom accidentally dropped scissors on my head when I was a baby. My mom had joked about this before, one of those exaggerated "When you were little . . . " stories that morph with every telling.

"Your mom felt so guilty!" her friend told me over the phone. This was just after she had died, and I was both hungry for and nauseous by any memory of her. "But it was just the blunt end of the scissors, the handle. You were totally fine. She always worried about it, though."

She did? Sure, she had mentioned the story, but it was always told with humor, so much so that I never actually believed the scissors made contact with my body. Hearing this from her friend led me to actually ponder how the moment must have gone: a young mom, nervous, tired, and alone in a new city on a weird coast. How had she managed? Made friends? Did she get overwhelmed and cry? Who was this woman, and what was she doing holding scissors near a baby anyway?

Nothing in my grief has hurt quite so much as becoming a mother without my mom present. Every second of pregnancy and parenting is tinged with the strange sensation that I can share none of it with my mother. And in a world where it's fairly common for people to die in their fifties and sixties, society still acts as if every woman has a (retired, in perfect health, and with nothing else going on) mother in their lives who will drop everything and help them once their kid is born. The second you get pregnant, you hear the question constantly: "Is your mom coming to help?" After almost ten months of this, I couldn't even force a fake smile to go along with my curt reply of "Nope! She's dead."

By the end of my first pregnancy I was exhausted, both by the 24/7 hiccups my baby was blasting onto my cervix and by the relentless reminders that my mom was not going to bear witness to this all-important life moment. Still, my husband and I signed up for a birthing class to, you know, get in the spirit of things. As we sat with the five other couples during our first session, squashed on couches in a small office in downtown Manhattan, it became clear that the class had a very specific focus: natural birth rules; all other birth drools. From week one, the teacher suggested that unmedicated child-birth was clearly the preferred manner of pushing babies out. Epidurals were touched on but in a condescending, scary tone. I wasn't planning on getting one, but I was definitely open to it, and this was not a particularly safe space for admitting that. And while C-sections were covered (thank God, because I ended up getting a rather catastrophic one), we spent most of our time smooshing our faces into yoga balls and moaning as our partners awkwardly pressed their clammy hands onto our lower backs. One session was devoted to a famous birthing video in which a dew-faced woman labors beside a river and compares her contractions to the sun's rays bursting forth. It ends with her pushing her new baby out in her beautiful, tiled Jacuzzi as her family—kids and all—floats alongside her. You know—exactly like what I was sure to experience at a birthing center in midtown Manhattan.

On our final night of the class, our teacher gazed out at us with her hands clutched, a "this is gonna be *SO* meaningful!" look in her eye. You know the look—it's the one someone gives before they begin a poetry slam. "So," she said. "I want us to go around and share what our support system will be during and after birth." She looked at us with an expectant look in her eye. "You know," she said, "like if your mom is coming to stay with you."

Anthony immediately looked at me, eyebrows raised. I knew what he was thinking. Anthony's mom also died when he was twenty-seven—very suddenly of a heart attack. Even worse, she died the day before Mother's Day, which is particularly cruel and horrible. If you mom dies Mother's Day weekend, you get double points on the Dead Mom Scale of Terribleness. His own experience meant he was unfailingly empathetic with mine. Turns out, being married to a fellow Dead Mom-er is a great relief in the moments when other humans are oblivious to the fact that moms die. And in case it wasn't clear before, I want to reiterate: Moms die. Moms leave. Moms get cut out of lives for good reasons. Moms are in poor health. Moms work. Moms live far away and can't afford a plane ticket. Not everyone has a mom, so for the love of God please stop asking pregnant, expecting, or adopting women about them!

I'd thought the practice of having your mom there with you during and after childbirth was antiquated, the stuff of *Mad Men*. Or I figured people would be more thoughtful with such questions, operating under the assumption that lots of us don't have moms anymore. Maybe, because I always knew my mom wouldn't be there, I'd created a reality for myself where I assumed this kind of stuff didn't happen. But as we slowly went around the circle of our birthing class, couple after couple detailed elaborate plans of mothers already staying with them, renting apartments to be nearby, or moving in for months at a time. Surely, I thought to myself, another person is going to reveal that they, too, are motherless and have scraped together a support system of friends, dads, stepmoms, siblings, and whoever else can hang around. But the constant theme of the night was Moms Moms Moms, older women abandoning their lives to rush to the side of their kids as they were about to have kids themselves. I pursed my lips and smiled as I listened, but my insides were moving in a familiar spiral. Maybe you know the one: when jealousy stabs you, and then grief pours salt into the wound, and then they both laugh and do it again and again and again. But what made it all worse was not just how jealous I was to be missing out on having my own Mom Helper, it was the prickly, irritated way so many women spoke of their mothers' arrival.

To hear others complain about their mom when yours is dead and not get pissed by it is an art form that requires such skill, they could teach it in Year 7 at Hogwarts. You must accept your feelings of resentment and irritation toward the complainers, while also understanding that they have every right to loathe their own moms. We all know that even the World's Greatest Mom (ahem, me) is straight-up annoying as hell sometimes. And some moms are so nightmarish and destructive that they're the sole reason people head to therapy each week. (My elementary school teachers are the ones who trashed my self-esteem, but to each their own trauma.) But for those of us who had relatively cool moms, their absence during your own transition into parenthood just adds a shiny layer of shit on top of everything else going on.

Soon everyone's eyes in the group were on us. Anthony tightened his grip around my waist, sensing that I was both almost in tears and holding in gas because we'd shoved burritos in our mouths just minutes before walking into the class. "Our moms are both dead," he said, teeth clenched. "We are mostly just going at it by ourselves."

Now would be a good time to clarify that we did not go at it by ourselves. In fact, we had a very solid, enviable support system. My dad and stepmom were very helpful and in and out during that first month, and Anthony's dad, stepmom, brother, and brother's then-girlfriend stayed for almost two weeks and literally nursed me back to health after the C-section and spinal headache* knocked me on my ass. Plus we had an army of friends feeding us, sending us gifts, and stopping by throughout those first few months. We were the opposite of alone. And yet her absence loomed over me.

When I was a (very attractive, totally cool, not miserable at all) teenager, my mom would playfully taunt me with her own father's words. "Grampy always used to say to me, 'Just you wait 'til you have kids,'" she would warn me when I was being my particular brand of moody asshole. "Just you wait."

---

* You might be asking yourself, "Hey, Kate, I know this is a book about dead moms, but, like, WTF is a 'spinal headache'?" And I am here to say, "Google it," because I do not understand medical ailments. But basically it's a thing that happens when spinals and epidurals go wrong, and it left my entire body feeling as if I had the world's worst migraine, whiplash, and vertigo all at once. It was fun!

And now here I am, with kids, and I can't tell her that she was right all along. That I know what she means now: that my kids are massive pains in my ass, but I love them more than the moon loves pulling the ocean back and forth without a break.

The first time I really understood how much my mom loved me, I was watching the Jennifer Lopez episode of VH1's *Behind the Music*. Wait, wait—stay with me on this. A running theme of the show is her sometimes rocky relationship with her strict mother, Guadalupe. Toward the end, Jennifer reveals that, after she had her kids, Max and Emme, her mom gave her a card. "The way you feel about Max and Emme," it read, "I feel about you."

"And I was like, 'Oh my God,'" says Jen. As I was watching this, I was also like, "Oh my God," because her blowout looked *amazing*. But also because it was the first time I ever realized that my mom loved me in the same fierce, relentless, unconditional way I love my own kids. Just like that, I got it. Thank you, VH1 and "Jenny from the Block."

And so I have plodded on in her absence, trying to piece together how to be a mother. Since starting off seething in that birthing class, I've slowly figured out a plan of action that I want to share with you, in case you, too, agonize over your mom's absence as you head toward parenthood. You ready for it? Here goes:

You already know everything.

Kate, certainly you don't mean . . . ?

Yes, yes I do. EV-ER-Y-THING.

This is the lasting gift of your mom—for better or for worse depending on where your mom ranks on the Asshole Scale.

She implanted in you the knowledge of how to parent, just by being *your* parent. I know this because my father, whose own mother hung a leather belt in the kitchen with which she'd threaten ass whoopings when my dad misbehaved (she rarely used it, but the threat was scary enough), never laid a hand on us. His childhood led him to raise us in the opposite way of his parents. He was a master at speaking at us in a stern, measured voice whenever he became angry, which was often, because let me tell you, my brother and I really maxed out our asshole cards. In fact I can only remember him raising his voice at me once, when I racked up $40 worth of overdue fees at the library in high school.

My mom's fingerprints are all over how I parent, popping up in ways I didn't even expect. The lullabies she sang to me came rushing out of my mouth the second my kids were born, as if someone turned on some sort of song faucet in my brain. The way I barge into their rooms first thing in the morning, singing to wake them up, which is the most horrific way to be shaken from your sleep. Little bits of her keep flying out of me, as if she's been trapped inside all this time and all it took were my kids being born for her to reveal herself.

Perhaps this is terrible advice (er, yeah, it definitely is, but here goes!): I did not read a single parenting book. I'm not a *total* monster—I've ordered them on Amazon, unboxed them, recycled the box, and then shoved them on a shelf without touching a single page. It's almost the same as reading!

Instead, I have followed my instinct and empathy, tuning into my kids and trying to decipher the best choices for them. And it turns out, memories of my mom's parenting suddenly appear when I'm in the middle of dealing with them, like a weird CNN hologram. This is what I lean on when I'm unsure of how to handle my numerous parenting crises. Is it as effective as texting her, "Hey, how do I get L to stop pooping in her pants when she's in her bed awake at nap time?" and getting an immediate response? No, of course not. (Also, anyone who knows how to get my four-year-old to stop doing this should contact me immediately. It is *really* gross.)

But I remember how she patiently read to us each night and how she gave my friend Rachel and me Smarties to distract us when we fought. Other times, when my kids are driving me so crazy I feel as if I could grab a plate and smash it against the wall, I think of the time my mom, my brother, and I were watching *Live Aid* on the couch, and she smacked my hand when I tried to steal my brother's popcorn. I remember that, in all her wonderful mom glory, she was human and imperfect (and probably so damn tired). And I know that no matter what I do as a parent with my daughters, I am, too.

Her illness and death also schooled me on how to mother, especially during the living nightmare of a time known as "bringing home a newborn," during which I did not shower and often ate dry ramen noodles as a snack in the middle of the night. Transforming from my mom's kid to her caregiver during her illness proved that I actually have it in me to care for and nurture someone else, with zero expectations in return. And if I could survive losing her, I could survive anything. Turns out, I learned how to be a mom by her being here but also by her leaving. Her life and death taught me more than any parenting book ever could. Not that I'd read it.

The Dead Mom Poetry Corner

For years, my mom clipped inspirational quotes from the *Boston Globe* and taped them to our refrigerator. There is one that has stayed with me, still, by poet Mitsuye Yamada:

What Your Mother Tells You
What your mother tells you now
in time
you will come to know.

Growing up, this poem always felt particularly condescending to me when she was alive, a haiku version of someone telling you, "You'll get it someday." But now as an adult, I see how right it is. You don't need to be a parent to grow into these words, though I have found them to be particularly poignant when it comes to parenting. Everything she told me about motherhood, even just through her actions, I've come to know. The most important being this: to parent well is to love unconditionally.

16

⸺⊱⸱⊰⸺

When Your Kids Ask

For someone who is addicted to the internet as much as I am, you would logically assume that I used it to Google "talking to kids about death" after my daughters were born. That one search alone hands you 97,400,000 results, more than enough information on how to approach the topic in a way that won't screw your kids up. Amazon even offers you over thirty-six different books on death from which to choose, for your kids and yourself. The internet has you covered, parents! Certainly I must have devoured this information, so that I could gently and appropriately introduce the idea of my dead mom to my kids with confidence and cool. Right?

Nope!

On the Whoops! I Screwed Up! parenting scale, I am off the charts.

Instead, I bounced my first daughter, Eleanor, in my arms and pointed at photos of my mom. She was a baby then, barely able to sit up on her own. But I spoke to her as if she got every word. "This is my mom!" I said, tapping my finger on a photo of my mom and me in a pink wooden frame. "Your grandmother Martha." Just talking about her made my eyes wet; my tears were like saliva, my eyes hungry for sadness. In one particular photo, we're eating soup outside of a Whole Foods on her fifty-sixth birthday. Her last birthday. I'm staring at the camera, she's clutching her hands and smiling, gazing off at something in the distance. She was thin with sickness, her hair a dull shade I can only describe as "cancer gray," because the disease and the chemo took her beautiful, dark, salt-and-pepper hair and killed it, too. But still, in that photo, she's the most stunning thing I've ever seen. I remember that day because it was a good one, the photo taken before things went from kinda scary to "Oh God, we're living in a nightmare from which we will never escape" bad. Other than her birthday it was a very boring day, which is what made it so special. There were no alarming fevers requiring trips to the emergency room or terrifying scans that spelled out bad news in black and white. We hit up her chemo appointment at Mass General, then lunch at Whole Foods down the street. Soup for both of us. Her friend Patty met us there, snapping pictures of us in between bites. Patty is an incredible photographer, someone who sees the moments that you will want to remember later, before they even become clear to you. My mom was in high spirits that day; the new chemo she was on had stabilized her tumor, and she was eating—in my mind, eating meant that the cancer was losing. Little did I know it would score a win a few weeks later, when she went into septic shock and landed in the ICU. But that day was perfect: cool but sunny, celebratory, full of laughter—a tiny triumph during a time of so much loss.

E leanor arrived in 2010, three years after mom's death. The second she showed up with her weird newborn mohawk and juicy cheeks, I was eager for her to know who my mom was, that she had existed and mattered and been so very real once. Eleanor was my first kid, and so of course I wanted to tell her all our stories—about my mom's gentle gaze and deep affecting laugh, our trip to Scotland when I was ten when we slept in the most comfortable twin beds, that time when I got dumped by my first boyfriend and she drove up from Massachusetts to my college in Maine to sit with me in my dorm room as I wept for hours in a beanbag chair. I wanted every experience I had with my mom to flow from my brain to hers, for her to see our life together like some sort of clairvoyant wunderkind in a Stephen King movie. So I simply started talking the second I thought she might understand. But I never took a second to ponder what came after. I never paused to figure out what I should say when she quickly figured out that the grandmother she calls "Steen" is not the one I kept pointing to in that pink picture frame. I should have known she'd piece it together quickly, what with my stepmom's red hair and accent. But I was operating on 100 percent emotion and 0 percent logic, which, if I'm being honest, is how I spend most of my days.

Later, when Eleanor was five and I had already ruined her, my close friend Nina would give me the sagest advice I ever heard about speaking to kids about the super hard, very bad things. Nina is a teacher, with decades of experience, and she has a gentle but matter-of-fact way of presenting you with the sometimes-brute force of life. She told me that if kids ask a

question, then you answer it honestly, but don't force information on them before they're ready.

Oops.

I had doomed myself. Eleanor is precocious and curious, with a memory that saves detail like a computer server.
Just as quickly as she could walk and take a dump in a tiny
plastic toilet shaped like a frog, she could also ask, "Where
is your mom?" This should have been my cue to Google, read
up, and research how to talk about death with kids. Instead, I
was paralyzed with fear of learning what the experts advised.
I was ashamed to admit why the thought of learning the
proper approach terrified me: I knew every book and website
would tell me that I was already handling this all wrong, that I
should have withheld this Dead Mom Info until she was older
and better prepared. That I only told her because I was selfish,
because my grief won out over being a good, responsible mom.

"Kate," I imagined the book with the sad, slumped-over
teddy bear on the cover would say, "You really screwed this
one up. Why can't you just learn to shut the eff up for once?"

But it was too late. I already had a toddler who knew too
much. Planting the knowledge of death in her tiny, developing
brain basically gave her the air of a goth teen who just figured
out that all of her musical heroes died thirty years ago, with a
little bit of obnoxious-guy-in-your-philosophy-class-who-won't-
stop-asking-questions-even-though-the-professor-is-clearly-
annoyed mixed in.

Around the age of three, she nonchalantly declared,
"Your mom is dead!" while we stood in line for grocer-
ies at Trader Joe's. It was the first of many such public
interrogations. I nodded confidently, attempting my best

mom-who-has-her-shit-together impression. But then she followed up with *"But where is she?"* My mouth stumbled over words, trying to explain the differences in people who believe in heaven (my in-laws) or people who don't (me). I tried to tell her that my mom believed in the laws of nature, above all, and if she looked hard she could find her there, somewhere between the branches, and the cracks of sunlight, and the smooth, green creases of leaves.

But most of the time I just answered honestly: "I don't know." Sometimes I cried.

In my excitement to tell my daughter about this woman who was a part of her, a woman who would have loved her and her sister unfailingly with every fiber of her body, I created a kid who was just as excited to talk about how dead she was. "Your mom is never coming back, and you can't hear her voice," she announced in the car. "My grandmother is dead!" she declared to the UPS guy dropping off my eight million Amazon purchases.

But despite all the badgering and the endless color commentary about death, it took her almost two years to ask *the* question. "Mom," she said one day at the ripe old age of five, strapped into her car seat behind me on our drive home from school. "How did your mom die?"

I knew this moment would eventually arrive, and contrary to my original Just Go for It! approach, by then I had done some reading on how to speak to kids about cancer, illness, and death. And I had taken Nina's advice to heart. But the question caught me off guard, still. I attempted some slow, yogic breathing, which we all know is bullshit in times of true, weepy hysteria. Not even the slowest inhale could stop the sob that crept up from my chest into the straining muscles of my throat. Something about having to actually reveal the truth to my kid—not simply about my mom's death, but of the sad ways of the world—devastated me in a way I hadn't considered before. I struggled with how to be honest without terrifying the crap out of her.

"Her body got very sick," I managed. "Not like when you get a cold. It's a different kind of sick that won't happen to you."

"*Liar!*" my brain shouted as it flashed to all the Instagram accounts I follow documenting beautiful children and their cancer battles, with hashtags like #prayersforAshley and #Morgansfight.

"It mostly happens to grown-ups when they're very old."

"*That's two for two!*" my brain shouted again, as it flashed up an image of my aunt Leslie.

"Because she got sick her body stopped working."

My brain finally shut up, and I hoped that this was enough—that she felt informed but also unafraid. Instead she loaded up her question gun and lobbed one more grenade at me.

"Is one day your body going to get sick and stop working?" she asked in her broken, preschooler English.

"Probably not," I replied, defeated. I couldn't bring myself to lie completely.

"But am I going to die?" she asked.

"Everything has a beginning, middle, and end," I said. "Including our lives. But you're just at the beginning. And the end won't happen for a long time."

She sat, quietly, chewing on my words. Finally, she piped up again: "Mom?"

I inhaled, preparing for the worst. "Yeah?"

"Can I roll down my window?"

I replied by pressing the buttons on the side of my door, lowering all four windows until the air was loud and roaring. We drove the rest of the way home in silence, the sun casting pink light on the mountains behind us.

Here is the awful truth behind all of these conversations: we all die. How pathetic is that? As parents, we're forced to somehow sell our kids on our mortality, making death seem like this thing that's not going to happen for "a very long time," but when it does, it won't be all that bad. And for parents with dead moms, the job is doubly tough, as we attempt to portray this awful thing that took a big dump on our lives as "okay!"

As much as "trigger" has become a catchall phrase in our cultural-speak these days, it's a legitimate, valid sensation. The world is full of Dead Mom Triggers (I cry at diaper commercials, okay?), but the double whammy of stumbling through explaining death while also explaining why your kid has no biological grandmother to write forced Christmas cards to each year is particularly rough.

I want my kids to know everything about my mom. But I also want them to know that what happened to her won't happen to me. They won't have to drain bags of bile and weep on the floor as I lay on the couch too tired to move, or cut a strand of my thin, gray hair off my head just minutes after I die, just to hold on to something.

But I can't promise this. I can't do anything. All I can do is fumble my way through the conversations, be open and honest when they ask questions, and gentle when they need reassurance. And in between this, I can help make the memories that they will share with their kids if I kick it at fifty-six. I scream too loud when they jump on the couch; I surprise them with Shopkins toy figurines even though they seriously perpetuate a culture of materialism and gender stereotypes;* we go for walks every time it rains in Los Angeles, jumping so hard in the puddles that no rain boots can protect us.

We exist, which is the best we can do while we're here.

As she's gotten older, Eleanor's public questions about death have subsided. Now a sophisticated first grader, she saves them for moments that catch me completely off guard, like when we were recently slapping cards down on the kitchen table in a heated Uno game. She paused in the middle of kicking my ass. "Your mom is dead, right?"

I nodded, trying to stay casual and chill. (This is hard for me.)

"But where *is* she?" she asked.

"Well," I said, "Your grandma Martha loved nature. So I like to think that every time I see a bird, I'm seeing her, too."

Immediately I began to second-guess my response. Too cerebral? Should I have gone with butterflies instead?

But Eleanor just nodded, as if I'd said the most logical thing in the world. "When I die," she said, nibbling on the edge of her lone card, "I'm going to become a bird."

"Me, too," I agreed.

She laid her last card down on the pile. Wild.

"I win!" she declared.

---

* If you've never heard of Shopkins, just imagine a tiny plastic lipstick figurine with winking eyes named Lippy Lip and shudder away.

I picked up the deck and shuffled the cards through my fingers. "Should we play again?"

"Yeah," she paused. "But Mom?" she said slowly. I gulped, and prepared myself for what was to come next.

"Yes?"

"My butt *really* itches."

Before I could reply, she peeled her body off of the wooden bench and marched toward the bathroom.

"I need to take a break," she yelled, shutting the door behind her, leaving me alone with a deck of cards in my hands, watching the birds fly by out the window.

ADVICE CORNER: MY TEACHER FRIEND NINA SCHOOLS ME ON HOW TO TALK TO KIDS ABOUT DEATH

I should have asked these questions before I had kids, but better late than never, right? My super-wise teacher friend Nina weighs in with these tips on how to do the Very Hard Thing: talk to your kids about death.

WHAT SHOULD YOU SAY WHEN YOUR KIDS ASK ABOUT DEATH?

I think, Kate, the most important thing is not so much what we say when children ask about death (it is hard for even the "best" to get that right spontaneously) but how we *physically* react. They need to see and feel our fearlessness in letting their questions into our lives.

Once children feel the coziness of welcoming conversation, we try to listen slowly in order to allow them to regulate the flow of information.

HOW DO YOU MAKE DEATH NOT FEEL SCARY?

Lifetimes: A Beautiful Way to Explain Death to Children by Bryan Mellonie (beautifully illustrated by Robert Ingpen).

Whenever I take this book from the shelves at school, the children know that an animal or person has died. The main message of the book is that all life has a beginning, a lifetime, and an ending, and it links looming, abstract questions to poignant, concrete answers with (in my opinion) beautifully and simply rendered (few) words and illustrations.

It is scary for a child to feel alone or "singled out" when sad/bad things happen. For children, generalizing comforts the personal. For example: "When animals die . . . When people die . . . When children experience the death of a pet . . . a person . . . "

The process of generalizing allows the personal experience of death (and other very hard things in life) into a child's reality as a less scary event because it is not concentrated just on her or him. So "my grandmother . . . " or "my dog . . . " doesn't feel like the scary "I."

WHAT'S A SIMPLE ANSWER TO GIVE THEM WHEN THEY ASK ABOUT YOUR DEAD MOM?

Physically pause, love-smile, bend eye-to-eye, and ask, "What would you like to know?"

Or, "Can you think of one (more) thing about my mom you would like to know?"

If "one more thing . . . " is a question a child asks more than once, it might be good (for both parent and child) to construct a book of grandchild-driven questions with a parent's answers. Building the life of a missed loved one from death back to birth can comfort a child's yearning to make the abstract of a person missing from his or her life into a concrete loved one.

———❧❦———

17

Saying Goodbye to Grief

I was cutting strawberries at the sink the other night, fully in my mom element, as Eleanor and Lydia bounced up and down at the kitchen table, waiting like impatient petting-zoo animals to be fed. I thought of my mother, standing over her own kitchen sink all those years ago, doing the same exact thing. Slicing fruit. I adored watching her slice fruit. She could skin an apple with one swift flick of her knife, tossing the peel on the counter like some sort of motherly mic drop. She'd blast through a container of strawberries in sixty seconds, holding the knife and fruit in the same hand, nimbly pressing the blade through the fruit's red flesh and up into her thumb without once cutting her own skin. I'd spent years clumsily slicing into strawberries on a cutting board, too scared of stabbing myself to try it her way. But over the years I'd gained courage from childbirth and a consistent Ativan prescription, and I started cutting strawberries just like her without even realizing it.

I've spent years grieving her death deeply (as if you can't tell from this book). But as I stood there the other night, going through *her* motions, I had an unsettling realization. As usual, I was conjuring up emotional images of my mother, a regular habit of mine for the last decade now. But this time, I felt no sadness, no tears, no urge to curl up in the fetal position at the foot of my sink. My grief was simply gone. And I didn't like it.

As the months and years ticked on after D(eath) Day, I became more and more comfortable with my grief. I even started to like it, like a toxic friend who is 90 percent an awful nightmare to be around but 10 percent so much fun to be around that you keep coming back. "Why do I like this person?!" you wonder when they've hurt you for the 19,805,397,340,824th time, and then they text you seventy-five heart emojis, and off you go to meet them at the bar. It's not that my grief was fun, but it was comfortable, like a hotel bathrobe just waiting to be slipped on anytime things got rough. At first, the grief clung to me, chasing me down like a serial killer in a horror movie. No matter where I went or what I did, the grief followed, lurking, ready to pop out in a bookstore or yoga class, or while I shout-sang karaoke with friends. But something somewhere shifted, and I became the one clinging.

"Get back here!" I screamed, tightening my grip on my sorrow. Holding on to my grief was how I held on to my mom. Feeling sad meant that I hadn't totally forgotten her, that she still existed, mattered, and lived.

But here is the awful truth about grief that no sad person really ever wants to admit: the old adage is true. Time sorta *does* heal things. It's been a decade now, and the rushing roar of pain and mourning that once swept me up and carried me away has now almost dried up to a trickle. You'd think I'd be pleased that my mental state could now return to its normal/ occasionally depressed/mostly still confused by the plot of *Lost* state. But when I realized that my grief was slowly dissipating, I turned into the living, breathing version of that beloved internet-memed photo of James Van Der Beek crying on *Dawson's Creek* (a show I have never actually watched—forgive me, fellow members of my generation). My mom was dead, for fuck's sake. The least I was owed was the safety of eternal sadness, right?

In that moment at the sink cutting strawberries, I pushed myself to go into my grief, to come up with a memory, a moment—something to hold on to, to bring her back. I searched my mind to hear the pitch of her laughter, to eye the slope of her shoulders as she sat paying bills at her desk, to watch her stand there cutting strawberries, piling them into the dingy plastic yellow strainer she bought before I was born. I wanted to feel the sadness because it would mean that a part of her was still there, living and breathing through my sorrow. But my mind just circled around and around until I finished my work, tossing the strawberry tops in the trash.

My grief slipping away feels just as terrifying as it did to lose her. It's as if I'm losing her all over again. My memories of her are becoming sloppy and unclear, foggy around the edges. I can still remember the sound of her voice, but her laugh— her pure, instinctive guffaw—is gone. *Gone.* I am so furious that it has left me, betrayed by my own brain. Sometimes I take out my mental shovel and dig around between my ears for the tone, the cadence of her laugh. But it's simply moved on, slipping away when I wasn't looking.

For years I've kept a box of Mom mementos shoved on the bottom shelf of my bedside table. What strange things we hold on to to keep the ones we love close. A single cotton sock. Her old tube of Vaseline lip balm that she kept by her bed and labeled "mom" in red Sharpie, so we wouldn't use it and pass along our germs. A pile of grocery lists from when she was sick, with items like "coffee ice cream—Brighams, cran juice, real oatmeal—not flavored" preserved in pencil. Together, these lists document her illness in handwriting alone—her sloping script becoming more and more scribbled and small as her cancer wore on. I use these things like talismans to bring me back in time; if I clutch and smell and cry all over them just hard enough, maybe I will relive her for one quick second. They never quite deliver on their promise, but I hold on to them anyway, just in case.

When I cry for her now—which I still do, though not as often—I cry for my grief, too. I want it back just as much as I want her. I want that raw sadness, because it delivers me back in time to a place where she's not been dead for over ten years. I want to be back in the throes of my sorrow, when even the simple of act of getting out of my bed to go to the bathroom hurt too much, simply because she was gone.

What does it mean, to move on? I know that I will never be "over" her death. Sometimes I still wake up in so much pain over it I can't work, choosing instead to spend the day wailing on the couch as my dog looks on with a mix of empathy, pity, and desperation for a walk. Even a decade later, the strangest moment can launch me into my sadness pool, where I flail around like a kid who never learned to swim and whose mom forgot to pack their floaties.

But most of the time, I feel beyond my grief, removed from it. I'm almost ahead of it now, beating it in its never-ending game of tag. Sometimes I push through life so fast that it's out of my sight completely. And then I realize that it's disappeared, and I panic. "Where are you?" I say to my grief. "Where are you?" I say to her.

I remind myself that she is dead but she is still here. She's there when I order sensible, secondhand—but perfectly fine, seriously!—Dansko clogs on eBay, even though they are the least cool shoe I could possibly wear out in public. She's there when I make her lentil soup recipe, without needing to consult the actual recipe card. And she lives on in my relationship with my daughters. She is there in the advice I give them about navigating friendships, in the songs we sing and the hugs we share, in my endless nagging to pick up their toys, put away their shoes. She's there when I'm at the sink slicing up strawberries for them to eat. I no longer need to drown in my sadness just to keep my mom alive. In letting go of my grief, I've found her in myself.

GETTING IN THE MOOD: FIVE POP CULTURE MUST-HAVES IF YOU'RE IN NEED OF A GOOD DEAD MOM CRY

Sometimes it just feels good to feel sad. And if your own grief isn't doing it, here are my top picks for guaranteed ugly cries.

THE FAMILY STONE

Ah, a romantic comedy featuring Rachel McAdams, Sarah Jessica Parker, Diane Keaton, and that timeless hunk Craig T. Nelson (you thought I was going to say Dermot Mulroney, didn't you?). What's not to love? This movie really messes with you because its premise is romance(!), but there's a dying-mom cloud hanging over the whole thing, lurking until it bites you in the ass right at the end of the movie.
6/10 Sobs

"THE BEST DAY" BY TAYLOR SWIFT

Go ahead, get your Taylor Swift jokes out now. Because the second you listen to TayTay's song about how much she loves her mom—complete with a music video of family-shot footage from her childhood—you will be a wet sack of sad bones. No, it's not about a dead mom, but it will definitely scratch that need-to-cry itch. Also this song is pure country-music Taylor, which we all know is the *best* Taylor. Sorry, 1989.
8/10 Sobs

HOUSES ARE FIELDS: POEMS BY TAIJE SILVERMAN

True story: I found this book while Googling "poems about dead moms" on a particularly hard, sleepless night during that first year without my mom. I stumbled on Silverman's beautiful poems, many of which chronicle her mom's cancer and death. This book is a salve for me and allows me to brag about reading poetry. Wins all around.
7/10 Sobs

THE LONG GOODBYE BY MEGHAN O'ROURKE AND THE MERCY PAPERS BY ROBIN ROMM

Two incredibly poignant, very hard-to-read memoirs about mothers dying. Read them back-to-back and you will enjoy hours of constant weeping.

9/10 Sobs

OTHER PEOPLE

About a year and a half after my mom died, I sat across a small table at a wine bar with my new friend, Chris. He had also just lost his mom to cancer, and we had exchanged a few emails about the madness of it all. We didn't really know much about each other, aside from our shared loss and some mutual friends. But we spent that night crying and drinking (and laughing! because why not?), and became quick friends. Fast forward eight years, and Chris is now the writer and director of this incredible movie, *Other People*, about—what else?—a mom dying of cancer and the family that surrounds her. Look, I hold a bias here because I am endorsing a friend's film, but if you want to both hysterically weep while also snort-laughing as snot drips out your nose, then this is the movie for you. I had to throw my contacts out after watching it because my potent salt tears obliterated them.

10/10 Sobs

18

What to Do When It's Not You

There was one thing I was certain of after my mom died: I was going to be amazing at supporting others after experiencing my own loss. Yep, surely my mom's death had turned me into some sort of grief rock star, who'd receive standing ovations every time I helped a fellow sad person. I was positive—cocky, even—that my mom's death had endowed me with great knowledge, wisdom, and relentless strength to offer others. *When someone I love goes through something like this,* I thought, *I'll know exactly what to do. I'm a* grief professional, *Goddamn it.*

I was almost downright eager for someone I knew to experience loss simply because I felt so prepared to help them. I would be a rock when they needed support and a shadow when they needed space and quiet. I would gently guide them through the worst of it with my humorous but empathetic handwritten notes and my healthy but filling casseroles. I would organize every food train. And I would police the people who didn't get it, like the ones who showed up needily for visits and somehow made someone else's tragedy all about them. Or the people who wanted to send flowers, not realizing they require work and die faster than you can say "thank you," and turn the cabinet under your sink into a vase graveyard.

And then, not quite two years after my mom died, a friend's dad was diagnosed with cancer. And suddenly, instead of suiting up in my Grief Superhero outfit and flying out the window with a lasagna in hand, I clammed up. I could not figure out how to help someone I'd known for years, someone who had been there for me when my own mom was sick. Instead I was paralyzed with a fear I think so many of us feel: WHAT IF I DO IT WRONG?!

I did not want to screw up supporting my friend, so much so I panicked over every little thing I did. Was my email too chipper? Did I not send enough cards? Should I text more? I couldn't figure out the right way to come through for her, and I was certain everything I was doing was wrong and offensive, annoying her more than it was helping.

A few years later, we got word that another friend's mom had died suddenly of a heart attack. Once again everything I tried to do felt strange, uncomfortable, definitely the wrong way of doing things. I bought a card and stared at it for a week, trying to find the right words to say. I was a writer and a Dead Mom haver; certainly I could come up with something better than "I'm so sorry for your loss," right?

(The answer is a big, fat no.)

Last year, my incredible, effortlessly hilarious, and unfailingly loyal friend Sam died from complications related to stage four lung cancer. (Since I may never get another chance to do it, I'd like to kindly say FUCK YOU to lung cancer.) And in the year of her diagnosis, illness, and death I was certain I was doing everything wrong. I wanted so badly to walk the line of being helpful without being too much, but I couldn't for the life of me figure out just how to do it right.

It turns out that living with a loved one's death does not magically shape us into awesome caregivers, friends, supporters, and food tree managers. In fact, sometimes it does the exact opposite. Going through that experience puts us more in our heads. Because we know too well that there's a learning curve that goes into being there for someone in the most appropriate way. And so I keep at it. I try and fail and try again. Because through this process of grief and sadness I have learned one thing: it's better to show up clumsily then not show up at all.

But wait, I've learned other things! And yes, I am now going to tell you all of them.

I

TAKE "ME" OUT OF IT.

Please notice how so much of my above-detailed panic was about myself. *I'm* doing it wrong! *I* don't know what to say! *I* don't want to impose! If this sounds familiar, please know that you're not a narcissist for thinking thoughts like this. (Fingers crossed that I'm not either; please remind me to ask my therapist.) You just want to do the right thing and not fail at it. But no one knows what to do when grief appears in their world, so we panic. First things first: stop worrying about what your response says about you. Know that the experience of supporting someone requires learning, and will involve missteps—no matter how many times you've done it before. No one's going to hold it against you. It is always better to do something than do nothing at all.

2

SHOW UP.

Do not disappear when someone you love is in pain. Do not make yourself small, or think that they won't want to hear from you. Be present. Express your support, your gratitude, and your empathy. It can be as small as a text message that says, "I am here for you. I'm with you." Don't shy away from the scary thing.

3

TRY NOT TO SAY, "LET ME KNOW WHAT I CAN DO TO HELP!" OR ASK, "IS THERE ANYTHING I CAN DO?"

These are the most well-intentioned words in the history of the English language, and yet they're also the least helpful. Has anyone ever heard these words and then replied, "Why yes, there *is* something for you to do!" Nope. Never. Not once. Because the person in need also doesn't want to impose on the person offering, and so nothing gets done. Instead try this. Make a list of things you could feasibly do to help someone and then offer a specific action: Walk their dog. Do their laundry. Do the dishes. Bring food. Clean out their fridge. Organize a food tree. Take out their trash. Regulate the flow of visitors. Help them move furniture. Pay for grocery delivery. Hire a cleaning service to clean their house. Water their flowers. Sit in their house just so they don't have to be alone.

Whatever it is, offer something. Anything! It can be small or grand, but it's up to you to figure out a thing you can do and offer it. And this can be hard. You might get nervous and worry— What if the person doesn't want the thing? Or like it? What if I am intruding or stepping into a space where I'm not welcome?

Know the boundaries of your relationship. Start small. And if you're really stuck, offer to sit with the person, make a list of the ways they could use some help, and then assign it to all the other well-intentioned people asking, "How can I help?"

4

DO NOT RELY ON THE GRIEVING PERSON
TO MAKE YOU FEEL BETTER.

A few years ago, psychologist Susan Silk wrote about her "ring theory" in the *LA Times*, in which the basic philosophy is this: The aggrieved person is the center dot, and every ring around her represents the people in her life, from closest (the inner ring) to random acquaintances from high school who post too many ultrasound pics on Facebook (the outer ring). Comfort, support, and help go in, toward the center, and all dumping goes out. No, you can't dump in.

In short: don't complain to the afflicted person about what's going on in their life. In shorter terms: don't be a dick. This seems incredibly simple, and yet here we are.

5

DON'T MAKE IT ALL ABOUT YOU.

When I was nine, my family made a pilgrimage to Disney World. It was there, on the walls of a cheap magic shop on Main Street, that I found a fake arm cast. I possess that strange mix of paralyzing shyness and relentless hunger for attention, and so I dragged my parents over and pointed at the cast until I left with it in a bag tucked under my arm. This was the only souvenir that I lugged home with me on the plane. (Screw the mouse ears—this cast was gonna deliver!) I returned to fourth grade sunburnt and with the cast on my arm, eager to convince my classmates that I had, devastatingly, broken my arm at Disney World. Please know that the cast looked nothing like an actual cast you would get at the hospital upon, you know, actually breaking your arm. It was bright white and smooth, like a mummy's arm, and completely open in the back, so you had to slide your arm in and then grip it against your stomach so as not to reveal that it was fake. It was also meant for your left arm, presumably because most people are right-handed and therefore it would be easy to wear the cast, "trick" people, and still get on with your life. Guess which idiot is left-handed? (Yes, Justin Bieber, but also: ME.) But I was undeterred and convinced that people would fall for it, especially with the signatures I scribbled on the cast to give it a more realistic feel. I was a performer, hungry for caring gazes and concerned questions from teachers and peers. Instead, the boy I had a crush on, the one with thick black hair whose name I am still too embarrassed to mention, walked up to me and asked, "Why are you wearing a weird fake cast on your arm?" I promptly ran to the girls' bathroom and hid it in the giant metal trash can.

What is it about illness and sadness that we're drawn to? Why do we want the attention that comes along with tragedy? Why does the gentle gaze of people who pity us feel so delicious, like rubbing lotion all over your skin, getting in your pajamas, and then taking a NyQuil even though you're not sick, just so you can fall asleep at eight PM? There's something hypnotic and addictive about receiving sympathy: it can feed our hungriest insecurities, so that we may not even realize we're chasing it. But lemme be clear: DO NOT MAKE SOMEONE ELSE'S ILLNESS ABOUT YOU. If you need to use a sob story to garner attention, adopt a rescue dog. (Just please take good care of it, and don't you dare take it back to the shelter because then you're part of the problem, Goddamn it.)

6

UNLESS THE PERSON REQUESTS FLOWERS, DO NOT BRING OR SEND FLOWERS.

Flowers should have a bad rep as a sympathy gift, because they die. But it's not that they're a reminder of loss that makes them so annoying; it's that they require work. And for a person dealing with a lot of other crap on their proverbial plate, flowers are the last thing they want on their to-do list. Imagine it:

"Oh, they're so pretty!" you say as the flower delivery guy hands over a giant vase full of flowers. You bring them into your kitchen and read the card, "awww!"-ing at the kind note. You pour the weird flower food into the vase. Then you spend a few minutes wondering if flower food actually does anything or if it's just a scam perpetuated by the flower industry, so you Google "flower industry" and go down that wormhole for another twenty minutes. Then the flowers die way sooner than you thought (Three days? Really?), but you let them sit out for two weeks, until the water is good and green. You finally decide that it's time to throw them out, but then you get busy and forget and three more days go by. Eventually, the swarm of fruit flies around them is so thick you don't have a choice. So you shove the flowers in the trash can, but the trash is full and the flowers are too long, so they stick out of the top of the trash can. Now you have to take out the Goddamn trash. When you get back inside, you stare at the algae-coated vase sitting in your sink. Your eyes travel over to your sponge. There's no way that sponge is gonna fit inside that vase, so you fill the vase with soap and hot water, hoping that will do the trick. But it doesn't, so that night, instead of going to bed, you wrap paper towels around the end of a wooden spoon, smearing the towels along the inside of the vase. But then the paper towels fall off into the vase and you can't reach them with a fork. So you decide to go to Ikea to buy new kitchen tongs to insert into the vase and pull the paper towels out. While you're there, you pick up a new coffee table because you've been meaning to get one anyway, and have you seen all the DIY Ikea hacks people post to the internet? Surely you can make something cool out of this coffee table. But then the coffee table doesn't fit in the trunk of your compact car, so you have to pay some man with a van to drive it back to your house, which feels creepy but you do it anyway, and then you're at home with your coffee table when you remember the whole reason you went to Ikea was to get a cheap pair of kitchen tongs to deal with the vase that's in your sink. But you forgot all about the tongs because you were so excited about the coffee table, so you drive back to Ikea, get the stupid tongs, drive home, notice all the dishes in your sink, do those first, and then, finally, use the tongs to get the paper towel out of the vase. Duh duh duh duhhhhh—the thing is clean! But you have nowhere to store it. So you shove the vase under the sink and forget about it, until the next time someone sends you flowers.

"Oh, they're so pretty!" you say.

And the cycle continues all over again. Trust me. I've, uh, done it before.

I was the recipient of so much kindness during my mom's illness and death that it eventually all blurred together into one big rainbow of love. So let me share some ideas if you're still not sold on the not-flowers idea. These are all very real, amazing things friends did for me:*

1. One friend sent me a care package filled with chocolate, lip gloss, romance novels, and a sweet note.

2. Friends joined together and bought me a gift certificate for a massage, which was a much needed escape from the Cancer House in which I lived.

3. An acquaintance knew of my passion for celebrity gossip and sent me an *Us* magazine from the 1980s in pristine condition. What a treasure! I still have it.

4. Friends drove up from New York City and flew in from California to surprise me along the route of my first half marathon. Other friends ran it with me. I felt very loved and supported, and I still cry when I think about it.

---

* I haven't said it enough: thank you, friends.

5. When I returned home to my New York City apartment after my mom died, a friend had snuck in beforehand and left me two beers and a Stephen King book on the Red Sox sitting on my windowsill. It was such a kind, simple gesture that I broke down weeping when I saw it.

It does not need to be big or fancy. A simple gesture goes a long way.

7

FOOD HELPS.

There is truly nothing more spectacular than not having to worry about how you are going to feed yourself when you haven't showered in three days because you're too busy dosing your mom up with morphine every two hours. Organizing a meal train is as simple as logging into a website, asking the person in need about their food preferences (no celery, please), and sending the site out to friends. This, above all, is the most helpful service friends can provide. And if you are unable to figure out how to turn on a stove or stack lasagna noodles, send takeout. Send a gift card. Leave a bag of chips on their doorstep with a note.

But whatever you do, don't equate a food drop-off with an actual visit. The one thing nicer than bringing someone food is bringing them food, leaving it at the door, and then getting the hell out of there. Chances are whoever is inside is in no mood to receive visitors. It's the only time in your life when ghosting someone is an acceptable way to treat them.

8
CHECK IN.

Text. Email. Let them know you're there, you're thinking of them, you see that they are dealing with something unimaginable and you love them, pain and all.

9
OFFER SUPPORT WITHOUT ANY STRINGS.

Sure, go ahead and text your friend-in-need a loving missive every day. But don't follow it with, "Hey, you didn't reply to my text. Did I do something to make you mad?" Now is not the time to expect anything in return from your friend in crisis. If you can't offer support without needing some sort of reciprocation from this person, then you should not offer them support to begin with. I beg of you, do not start friendship drama, or get needy, with someone going through #someshit. It is the cruelest thing you can do to someone who's suffering.

10
RESPECT THEIR CHOICES, EVEN IF *YOU* DON'T GET IT.

My mom was very private about her illness, like, in a way that even introverts would probably find weird. Toward the end of her life she wanted to be alone, with her immediate family only. She wasn't the kind of sick person who was receiving visitors on the day she died. She retreated; she needed quiet and calm to go.

She also requested a private, family-only funeral. She was loved by a network of friends that you could trace all over a map of the United States. And yet the thought of hordes of people coming together just for her overwhelmed her. "I just want it to be family," she insisted. We had a party in her honor a few months after she died, inviting friends to come sip wine and eat hors d'oeuvres in her name. But for a long time I felt incredibly guilty that her friends and some family members had been excluded from her funeral.

It can be incredibly difficult to respect—and execute—someone's wants when they simply don't make sense to you. But this is your job as their loved one. You don't ask why. You just do it.

II

SEND A CARD.

It is the most basic of gestures. When someone is suffering, is grieving, has lost a loved one, or is dealing with a shitty hand from the card game of life, send a card. If you don't know what to say, buy a card that says it for you and simply sign your name. And yes, texts and emails and Facebook messages are nice, but there is no replacement for a card sent in the mail. It's a simple, easy gesture that actually says a lot. Even if it feels weird or foreign, force your body to stand in front of the card aisle at Target, pick whichever one feels most appropriate, and drop it in the mailbox. And if your mom was anything like the thank-you note queen who raised me, she would definitely approve. That is reason enough to do it.

One gift you have most likely gained from your own loss is a deep empathy for others experiencing their own pain. If you feel you have no idea how to help someone in need, let the memory of your own experience guide you. The reason I know to make spaghetti pie for every food train I'm in is because someone made it for me, and the warmth and comfort it provided has stuck with me ever since. (Literally, too: that gooey deliciousness went straight to my ass.)

You already know what to do. The hardest part is just doing it. Go forth and conquer with kindness.

WHEN IN DOUBT: SPAGHETTI PIE!

Look, this is the easiest thing you could possibly make for a friend, *ever*. And it's delicious! There are lots of recipes available online, but I am going to try to make this as easy as possible. When I make this, I literally just throw it together. Cook it up, drop it on a friend's doorstep, and voilà—you've helped!

SHOPPING LIST:
- disposable deep-dish pie pan
- box of spaghetti

- jar of tomato sauce
- 1 egg
- Parmesan cheese
- shredded mozzarella cheese
- ground beef or turkey (optional, for meat eaters)
- peppers and spinach (optional, for vegetarians)
- (If you really want to go crazy, pick up a loaf of frozen garlic bread and a bag salad that comes with the dressing packet inside. It's a complete meal!)

Sauté some ground beef or turkey (or live it up and do both!) in a frying pan with onions. If you don't have onions, try a few shakes of onion powder. Or nothing at all. If you're going the veggie route, sauté away now, too.

Oh, and preheat your oven to 350 degrees.

While you're doing this, boil a pot of water and toss in the box of spaghetti. Follow the directions on the box, but cut your cooking time a minute or two short. The pasta should be al dente, because you're going to bake it, and that will cook it further.

When that's done, drain the pasta, run it under cold water, and put it in a bowl. Mix in the egg and sauce. Then throw in your cheese. I'm gonna let you eyeball this, because we're keeping it real loose and casual with this recipe. But save some mozzarella to go on top.

Grease your pie pan with some olive oil.

If you want to keep things extra simple, just mix in the meat or veggies with your pasta and dump it all into the pie pan. If you're going for the advanced technique, try some lasagna-like layering: meat, pasta, meat. Either way, top off your pie with some mozzarella.

Cook uncovered in the oven for thirty minutes or so. Or write the baking instructions on a piece of tinfoil, cover the pie, and let your friend do the cooking at their house. Just remember to turn off your oven.

19

━━⟨⊙⟩━━

Everything Happens

A few years ago I went on a women's retreat in Ojai, California, which if you've never been, is a place that looks exactly like a town full of women's retreats. It is earthy and warm, the cacti are plentiful, and every house has wooden beams and steer skulls looming over the fireplace. You roll into Ojai and suddenly find yourself using the word "succulent" a lot, whether it is to describe the weather, the food, or, you know, the succulents. I signed up for the trip because I was stuck: creatively, professionally, and emotionally. And, real talk: my astrologer, who was leading the group, is one of the most amazing, helpful women I've met in my life, and I'd follow her anywhere. The second you meet her she puts every stereotype or misconception you've ever had about astrologers to bed. She looks like the kind of mom you spot at a PTA meeting and immediately identify as the cool, down-to-earth mom you want to be friends with. She is warm like the sun, and I use this exhausted cliché here because in her case it's true.

It was an auspicious weekend full of creative, inspiring women downward dogging, reading poetry, and talking

243

earnestly about moons rising in Scorpio. Everyone was kind, open, and lacking in judgment of any kind. I ate a lot of perfectly ripe figs, went for healing swims late at night, and used the word "transformative" to describe everything from collaging to chimichurri sauce (it remains the best I've ever tasted). At one point I spoke to a lizard perched on a rock as if it were my mom. I journaled. I was INTO IT. But there was one thing that kept coming up for me throughout the weekend that hit that weird nagging spot in my stomach. Everything felt like it was happening for a reason: the new friendships that felt years old, the meaningful conversations, the poems read aloud that resonated so deeply they moved me to tears. Hell, I had almost even uttered those words a couple of times to women in the group. But there was a problem—I *loathed* that phrase. Hearing it out loud made me physically recoil. Up until that magical Ojai weekend, "Everything happens for a reason" had held that number one spot on my Most Hated Phrases of All Time list. And there I was, dancing dangerously close to the edge of becoming someone who *believed* it. The horror!

There's no one kind of person who drops "Everything happens for a reason." I've heard it from all sorts of people—evangelical Christians to Kundalini yoga fanatics to the lady checking me out at the Dollar Tree. Most often it comes right after I tell people about my mom's death. They get really confident, and even a little smug, as if they're letting me in on their family's secret chocolate chip cookie recipe. "Well," they say, giving a sassy, knowing tilt of their head, "I believe everything happens for a reason."

I'd respect this concept more if they followed it up with something like, "So yeah, Kate, your mom died so you will always have something to write about at two in the morning while crying alone listening to Celtic music." But no reason is ever actually put forth. It's just optimistically assumed that one day, your suffering and misery will pay off with some spectacular "reason" that makes it all worthwhile.

Of all the well-intentioned but totally offensive things people say after your mom dies, "Everything happens for a reason" is the one that always leaves me with a permanently clenched jaw. (Though "She's in a better place now" is a close second!) It is a passive justification of horrible things. It shows denial and an unwillingness to sit with the uncomfortable realization that sometimes shit literally just happens. Like when I was twenty-two, and I let a musician I was *verrrrrrry* casually dating long-distance—and whom my roommates and I immaturely nicknamed The Mormon after his former religion—and his grungy guitarist friend crash at my apartment in Brooklyn, only to wake up the next morning to discover that one of them had taken a shit in our kitchen sink.* When I confronted them, they both denied it, to the point where *I* began to feel bad for accusing them of something they most certainly did do. I felt *so* bad that I went out and bought the children's book *Everyone Poops* and gave it to The Mormon, to apologize for accusing him and his friend of taking a shit in my kitchen sink, which they *definitely* did. It's been thirteen years, and I'm still holding out for a reason on that one.

It's easy to understand *how* things happen, but it's the *why* that makes it hurt. Why did I spend forty dollars to keep

---

* This is the grossest thing to ever happen to me, and I once had to pull over while driving so both my kids could vomit simultaneously in a library parking lot.

playing the Kim Kardashian Hollywood game on my iPhone, and why did a cartoon character named Jaden, who looks like Justin Bieber with blue hair and bad taste in necklaces, break my digital heart? Why did a functioning adult think it a good idea to place their feces next to my dirty dishes? Why did cells mutate in my mom's pancreas and spread to her liver and cause her body to self-destruct? Certainly not so she would suffer miserable, excruciating, emotional, and physical pain for nine months and then die before she could see Obama become president or learn what an Instagram influencer is.

It's not as if I haven't hunted for answers or tried to find beauty and meaning in my loss. I've made new friends, found strength inside that I never knew existed, wrote a book solely about my Dead Mom Sads. But these aren't reasons. They don't justify her death. They're just the end result of my grief. If you pour enough water on dirt, something eventually blooms.

During that weekend in Ojai, everything felt aligned, as if life were a perfect stack of moments that fit neatly on top of each other. But it wasn't until our last day together that I came the closest I've ever come to being a full-blown Everything Happens for a Reason believer. We had been asked to bring a gift—something special from our own life—to exchange on our last day. I had grabbed a small crystal heart a friend gave me after my mom died. After a few hours with the other participants on our first day together, I knew immediately whom I wanted it to go to: Mary, a warm, easeful woman who was focused on calling love into her life.

(Look, I know how cheesy this might sound to some of you more cynical people out there, but remember: *it was a women's retreat in Ojai.* There was a lot of energetic, healing dance happening. This is the stuff I live for, and I was in my element.)

On our final day, we drew names for the gift exchange randomly, by pulling cards off the ground. And wouldn't you know it? When the time came to exchange gifts, whom did I have but Mary herself. And on her card? *My name.* She was sitting right next to me and handed me a necklace she had once bought herself as a symbol of strength and self-confidence following a time of grief—just the things I'd been desperately searching for. I wept the entire time, and for one second I felt as confident as those people who'd assured me before: maybe, just maybe, everything *does* happen for a reason.

Or maybe nothing happens for a reason. Or everything happens for no reason. Or perhaps it's just this: Everything happens. And that is good enough.

———

FIVE TERRIBLE* THINGS THAT HAVE HAPPENED IN MY LIFE THAT ARE STILL WITHOUT REASON (BESIDES THE BIG ONE)

- In the fourth grade, I ran outside for recess and fell on the pavement, scraping both my knees. My crush approached, and I thought he was going to bend down and offer his hand (in marriage! I was a weird, romantic nine-year-old). Instead he looked at me

---

* I'm using this term lightly here. My life has mostly been a walk in the park.

with disgust and announced, "Kate tucks her shirt into her underwear," and walked away with our very pretty, permed classmate. He was right: I did tuck my shirts into my underwear. He never did propose to me either.

- In college, I was passionately making out with a guy I was casually dating in his tiny dorm-room bed. I whispered, "I really like you," and he whispered back, "I really like you, too, Jane."

- This same guy dumped me over our summer break by never returning my calls. A year later, my group of friends went to his house—on an island, reach-able only by ferry!—for a long weekend. (We stayed friendly. It was a small college, and he had a cool house on an island—what can I say?) I accidentally left behind my journal, in which I had detailed what a shithead he was in numerous entries. I got the journal back months later. He'd definitely read it. I know this because he later drunkenly apologized for the many specific charges I laid out in my journal.

- When I was ten, my favorite band, New Kids on the Block, did an appearance on a local Boston talk show, *People Are Talking* (hosted by Tom Bergeron!). I set the VCR to record while I was at school. But my brother, who got home earlier than I did, took out my tape to watch a Disney movie, and it did not record. I cried for two days. I did not get to see this interview until I was thirty-one and found it on YouTube.

- I once got bedbugs. Enough said.

—◆◆◆◆◆—

20

You Go Girl

"**S**omeday you have to write about all the gifts," my mom joked from the passenger seat of her own car. We were driving home from the mall, speeding down Route 9 as a rainy, dismal Massachusetts day blurred by through the windows. We'd just gone to the mall on a mission to buy her some Uggs; she'd lost so much weight that she was cold constantly, and wool socks just weren't cutting it anymore. Every time I drove her somewhere, she insisted on buying me something, a token of appreciation for simply just showing up, steering the car, being her daughter. I'd been home for about six months now, and the gifts were piling up: new white corduroys, a grapefruit-scented Jo Malone candle, a bottle of Annick Goutal perfume.

In the moment I knew what she was suggesting: that I write up some blog post about all the things she'd bought me. She was teasing; my mom was never one who needed accolades for an act of kindness or a job well done. But when she said those words, my head spun. I wanted to tell her: there are *so* many gifts. Getting to spend days with you like this, just going to the same stupid mall we've been coming to since I was seven. The laughter, the red-eyed crying, the blunt and honest conversations about life and death. The fact that she was still here, next to me, weak and battered with tubes coming out of her stomach, but here.

Those were the real gifts that day. And there have been the gifts that followed after she died: a deeper appreciation of family, friends, and my daily existence; a greater awareness that suffering is universal; an understanding of her unconditional love of me through my unconditional love for my kids; a newfound adoration of romance novels and fan fiction to soothe all things sad. (*Twilight* fan fic heals—what can I say?)

But look, I'm also an incredibly materialistic, greedy person who still sends Christmas lists to her dad (and in-laws!) every winter. I like things, and I've never shaken my lust for presents, for physical objects that reward struggle or are purchased just because. And without my mom here to do the job, I started giving things to myself. And boy, did writing a book become a big justification for nonstop present shopping. Oh, Pilates classes? Yes, of course—I'll need the core strength to sit at a computer all day. A dress from Madewell that makes me look like a five-foot-ten tent made out of my grandmother's best tablecloth? But of course, a girl's gotta dress up once in a while—especially while sitting in front of a computer in her garage on a foam donut, because some of us got hemorrhoids after pushing a kid out. I could justify anything I put on the grocery store conveyer belt— baby wipes! burrito bowls! *Oprah* magazine!—simply because I was spending a lot of time thinking and writing about my mom, and that was hard. Woe is me, poor lil' baby Kate Spencer.

Enter: the Necklace. It was one of those pretty, delicate pieces of jewelry just about every women's magazine has decided you need to make up your #dreamcapsulewardrobe. It had a long rectangular pendant that was perfect for engraving. If you're a mom in your thirties who enjoys *The Bachelor* and shopping for leggings at Target at eleven PM on a Tuesday night (call me—you're my soul mate, and we need to hang), then this spot is typically reserved as a space to commemorate your kids. Maybe you engrave their initials, names, or birthdays, or if you're really deep, the latitude and longitude coordinates of the places they were born. Not me. Nope, I was going to get this necklace and engrave it with a message that honored my mom.

I sent my friend Megan a private Facebook message. She works for the jewelry company Stella & Dot* and had been posting on Facebook about the necklace, and she very graciously helped to arrange the order for me. My job was simple: I hopped on their website, selected the necklace, and typed in the words I wanted engraved, triple-checking them to make sure they were right. I knew exactly what I wanted printed on the shiny piece of gold, checked the words for ten minutes straight to make sure they were right, and then confirmed the order, sending them out into the ether until they landed back home on my neck: *You Go Girl*.

This simple phrase had been a rallying cry between my mother and me that crescendoed during her illness. In my twenties, she spent many a day counseling me over email about everything from my flailing career to my relationships to my general "everyone's life is going great but mine" quarter-life crisis. Surely she rolled her eyes as she read my frantically

* Stella & Dot is not a sponsor of this book, but if it wants to send me one thousand baubles for this mention, I will eagerly accept and wear them all at once.

typed out manifestos, but she always had a firm but cheery reply. She always capped her emailed pep talks with a simple "You go girl," followed by seventy-six exclamation points.

So when she was diagnosed with cancer, I "You go girl!"-ed everything: chemo sessions; her panicked, late-night emails fueled by steroids; the awful waiting period after a scan. When I brought her food in bed, I'd shout, "You go girl!" to persuade her to swallow the high-fat milk shake I'd made in an attempt to fight her cancer-induced weight loss. We "You go girl!"-ed each other so much that I got the words stitched onto a sweatshirt for her for that last Christmas. We stopped calling each other Mom and Kate, and simply started using "girl," and when she slipped into a comatose state near the end of her life, I laid next to her and whispered, "It's okay, girl—you can go."

For ten years I've shouted the words at myself in her absence when I needed confidence, support, or help—whether it's getting through childbirth or determining if I should go animal style on my burger at In-N-Out. (Yes. Always yes). So it only seemed fitting that I should engrave these words onto a necklace, something physical I could touch and wear as I wrote page after page about dealing with her death. It felt so perfectly symbolic that I was delightfully smug about it.

I hit "confirm" on my necklace order and then paced my house for four days, waiting for it to arrive. When the package finally landed on my doorstep, I "oohed" with delight. Finally, my mom's words would be around my neck for good! I yanked it out of its pretty packaging and peeked at the necklace. "Goddamn it," I grumbled, loud enough for my kid to hear and shout, "Don't use bad words!" at me from the playroom a few feet away. The lettering on the word "girl" was so close together it almost looked like "grl." I summoned my husband, who was washing dishes, to take a look.

"Can you read what this says?" I asked.

"Yeah," he said, with the self-assured tone of a middle-aged man who still does not need glasses. "Yo go girl."

"What? No, it says, 'You go girl.' The font must be too small."

"Kate." He sounded like a college professor arguing with a freshman about philosophy. "It says 'Yo go girl.' Look at it."

I yanked the chain from his hand and gazed down. Sure enough, in the tiniest letters, were the words "YO GO GIRL."

"Crap! They must have screwed up." I raced over to my phone and scrolled through my emails and order with Megan. Surely the person who took my order or made my necklace must have made a mistake. Human error is just part of life, right? I recently got a Britney Spears–esque French manicure; I get how mistakes happen. The email popped up on my phone. There, glaring up at me through the fingerprint-smudged iPhone screen, was the order I had placed. It was cold, hard evidence that I had, indeed, asked for my necklace to say "YO GO GIRL." Turns out, *I* was the human error.

"Oh no," I groaned. "How the hell did I write it wrong?" I had obsessively checked my order numerous times to ensure it was typo free. They should have sent me a necklace back that said "Dumb Idiot" on it. "I can't wear this," I said, crushed. This necklace was supposed to be an extension of my mom and our shared message to each other. Now it felt meaningless.

Anthony stared at me in that way he does when he's trying to be supportive but has no clue what I am so worked up about. "Why not?" he asked. "It still says something." He wandered off to leave me alone in the kitchen with my bougie problems.

He was right: it did still say *something*. And maybe, I reasoned to myself, it said something even better than "You go girl." I fastened it around my neck because it was too pretty not to wear and, you know, it was final sale, so no backsies. And strangely enough, as the days rolled by, I found myself reaching for the chain around my neck and saying the words to myself whenever I needed a pep talk. It was a direct answer to my often indecisive, wishy-washy worrying ways, like that good friend who tells you exactly how much they hate that weirdo you're dating, as opposed to the ones who force a smile and say, "They seem . . . nice."

Here's the thing about "Yo go girl." It's not a peppy, upbeat suggestion, like "You go girl." "Yo go girl" is insistent, a demand, an order. In my head I hear it like this: "Yo! Go Girl!" It's no-nonsense, in your face; there's no question about whether or not you're going to "go," because "Yo go girl" doesn't give you a choice. It doesn't allow you to back out or question things or reconsider. "Yo go girl" shoves you back to standing no matter how badly you want to fall.

Why am I telling you a stupid story about something as irrelevant as a misprint on a necklace I bought for myself as a present, when I don't really deserve any presents at all? Because I want you to think of these words when your grief starts to play the role of toxic best friend in your life. Though gendered, "Yo go girl" is a nonbinary message. You don't need to identify as a girl to "Yo go girl" yourself. Let it be your pep talk, too, no matter which way your gender swings.

I've had time to figure out some thoughts on grief. Er, just two thoughts. One is that it never ever completely goes away; it sticks with you, like a wart or an extra-large T-shirt you got in college and have worn to sleep in every night since. You can avoid grief, but it will eventually track you down and stick its middle finger right in your face, just when you thought you'd evaded its reach. And second: time moves forward, no matter how hard you drag your heels. Neither of these truths is pleasant, and surviving them—the eternal touch of grief and the undeniable march of time—requires some grit. Turns out, you can't just "You go girl" your way through it. You need the firm push of "*Yo* go girl" to face your grief head-on.

So onward I go without her, even though it still feels nightmarish at times. I make direct eye contact with my grief; I do not fear the endless forward movement of the hour hand on my clock. I simply go, and go, and go, because no matter how much time slips by, I will never lose the essence of her love pushing me forward, nudging me toward people, toward life, toward love, toward action, toward myself. And that—*that* is the gift.

Ten Things My Mom Said to Me Throughout My Life That Never Made It onto a Necklace (with Good Reason)

- I found the beers in the trunk of your car.[*]
- Your teacher sent a note home that your class is starting to smell, so I bought you some natural deodorant.[†]

---

[*] Guilty as charged.
[†] I was nine. *Nine*. And my B.O. was *rancid*.

- It's totally normal to have pubic hair at your age.*
- Is this marijuana?†
- Your dad and I are just concerned that you're not trying hard enough.‡
- I just don't understand how someone could fail gym.§
- If you get your tongue pierced, don't plan on coming home for Christmas.¶
- There's nothing wrong with being an intensely emotional and sensitive person.**
- I'm glad you broke up with him. He was an asshole.††
- Please call your mother.‡‡

---

* I was also nine. Fourth grade was rough.
† It wasn't. It was a spice mix my friends and I tried to smoke. We did not know where to score the real stuff.
‡ This could be applied to numerous situations throughout my life.
§ And the answer is: I never went. That's how.
¶ I *think* she was kidding, but I never tested her to find out.
** I really hope she was right.
†† She was definitely right.
‡‡ God, how I wish I could.

21

The Essence of My Mother

I was frantically searching a basket of junk in my bedroom when I found it. The whole reason I was even in there was to try to find a book of poems that had comforted me after my mom died.* I was on a break from writing this book and needed something to clear my head, wipe out the frenzied thoughts in my brain. Instead, I picked up a folder of old emails, the one I'd discovered while going through my mom's things a few years earlier. She'd filed away every email and Instant Message conversation she'd had with my brother and me while we were in college. I'd read every single one, and copied and bound them for my brother as a gift that Christmas. They were mortifying but a treasure. We both were entitled and whiny and used terrible grammar. She was positive and patient, if not a little naggy.

---

* Taije Silverman's *Houses Are Fields*, which I mentioned in Chapter 17. It's so good I'm telling you about it twice.

I'm not even sure why I opened the file—obviously the book of poems was not wedged in between the pages of me asking for money and complaining about my boyfriend. But I did, and that's when I noticed a page I'd somehow never seen before. I can't explain it, but there it was. It was a photocopy, and I don't know where the original is or if it even still exists. Two pages of my mom's handwriting had been stapled together; chunks of her work had been scratched out. It looked like an essay, and in the top left corner I could make out a title: "I Will Miss the Essence of My Mother."

It's dated 1998, nine years before both she and her mom would die. And her words capture exactly the same thing I was writing about as I worked on this book: the naiveté of childhood. The realization that your mother's spirit seeps into your whole world. The fear of losing her. The understanding that she exists forever in your own actions.

I ugly cried all over the thing. It was eerie, and beautiful, and timely, and maddening, and wonderful, all at once. Every single word felt like its own entire world of truth. And I knew just what she was trying to say. I mean, I wrote a whole damn book about it. Somehow, her short essay felt way more effective and to the point.

So I leave you with her words exactly how she wrote them, along with this simple fact: these feelings of loss and sorrow and deep, soul-crushing love are universal and unifying. They're in her and you and me and whoever comes next. They are what keeps us connected, no matter where we go. This essence is what we have left, and what we carry and pass on. You can never lose it, no matter how deep your loss. God, how I miss the essence of *my* mother. But I think what she was trying to tell me on this page is that she's never left me. She's in me. I'm stuck with her. And this is what unites all of us in the Dead Moms Club, besides just the obvious. Our mothers may be gone, but the essence of who they are is in us. And that is forever.

I Will Miss the
Essence of My Mother
Martha Spencer

August 1998

One thing I remember about my mother (and there are many memories) is that she was always there. I could go off no matter what my age, and when I came back she was there.

As children we roamed all around the woods or to friends' houses. Not a care in the world. It was not until I was older and had my own children that I fully felt the impact of her being there. Now I think I can feel some of the same things she experienced each time we left the house. Little did we know the anxiety she must have felt, wondering where we were and what we were doing. We would explore the woods behind the Stone Barn and sneak inside sometimes; go behind Calhoun House, be all over the Commons (the pool, the building, the cemetery). We would come home never fully knowing how she felt. Later I went to boarding school, and when I came home for my first T-day, she was there. The warmth that came from the house was her presence. Then college, again I'd come home, and she was there.

My children were born, and she was there with me . . . to SF and NJ. I could call and she always helped.

So now we do not have the physical being, but we have what she gave to our souls. We gained so much strength and knowledge and experienced so much through her interests.

I will miss the essence of my mother. It is up to us, her children and grandchildren, to carry this on, because if we do this, then she will always be there.

Acknowledgments

It is both exciting and terrifying to be given a blank space to thank all the people who made this book possible. I will almost certainly forget someone, and just the thought of this has given me enough anxiety to last a lifetime. My apologies, in advance, to the wonderful people I'm surely neglecting to mention. Please know I'll feel guilty about it forever!

Holly Root, you are an extraordinary agent, a true friend, and a calming, practical, thoughtful voice of reason and wisdom. I would not be here without you. I cherish your existence in my life.

Stephanie Knapp, thank you for getting me and this book, and helping to shape it into something real and readable. From the moment I perused your Twitter profile, I thought to myself, "I want this woman to be my editor!" and I am so grateful that you are. Your editorial prowess and encouragement have been invaluable.

Enormous thanks are in order to everyone at Seal Press, especially Kerry Rubenstein, who designed this beautiful cover, production wizard Amber Morris, and publicity genius Sharon Kunz. A big heap of gratitude to Beth Wright of Trio Bookworks for her copyediting skills.

Doree Shafrir, this book would not exist without you. The end. Thank you for your constructive feedback, words of encouragement, and endless laughs over various avocado toasts around LA.

Thank you, Lynn Shattuck, Susannah Becket, and Elizabeth Laime for reading various typo-laden iterations of my proposal and manuscript and offering your thoughts, support, and punch-ups.

To the Upright Citizens Brigade Theatre on both coasts and my ever-growing family of friends there: You are the best thing to happen to my life besides the obvious (my kids and *Laguna Beach*, season one). You are the funniest people I know, and the most loyal, kind, and supportive, too. I will never forget how the UCB community had my back during my mom's illness and death. Thank you.

Thank you to the many editors who have supported and published my work and helped me shape my voice as a writer. Special shout-out to Matt Muro for giving me my first, real, full-time writing job and being an all-around awesome editor, boss, and friend.

My friends. My amazing friends. I would truly be nothing without you. To my Dana women and my Bates women: You are my sisters. I don't know why you put up with me, but I'm so lucky that you do.

Liese Brown, you are the roommate of my life. Thank you for reading bits and pieces of this thing along the way and talking me out of numerous panic attacks (which you've been doing since the day we met).

Temple and Bradley Brighton helped watch my kids as I hammered out the first words of this book, and gave me a peaceful space to live and write in Boston for a week. I am so grateful to you both for your never-ending support.

John and Susan Brighton and John Breen and Susie Brighton have offered their unconditional support, love, and humor since the day I showed up on this earth, and have been my cheerleaders through this writing process. And to my extended families on both the Spencer and the Brighton sides: Thank you. I am so proud to be genetically connected to you all.

Much love to Christine Wallace, stepmother extraordinaire. Thank you for being part of our family story; I am so glad we get to claim you as one of our own.

John and Raelene King: I could not ask for better in-laws. Thank you for your love and support and beef stroganoff.

Andrew: Even though you got all the athletic genes in the family and the Italian skin that never sunburns, I still love you. Thank you for letting me share our experience in this book (and for reading it and giving it your blessing). I am proud to be your sister, and I am sorry I tormented you with a terrible nickname for most of your childhood.

Dad: I have given you a hard time since the moment I could talk, but the truth is you're just the best person I know. Everything I know about loving unconditionally I learned from you. Thank you for being open to me sharing about our family, and for your thoughtful, detailed edits and notes on my manuscript. Most importantly, thank you for letting me quit clarinet lessons in the fifth grade.

Eleanor and Lydia: You are my everything. I hope you don't need a book like this for a long, long time.

Anthony King: There are really no words to express how grateful I am that you're my partner in life. I am the luckiest.

To the many people who have reached out to me about their own dead moms (or dead people)—thank you for reading my words and sharing your own stories of loss with me. Being in the Dead Moms Club sucks, but it helps knowing I'm not alone.

Many people supported and helped my family and me during my mom's illness and death. I could say thank you until the end of time, and it still would not be enough.

The doctors, nurses, and staff at Massachusetts General Hospital are herocs. Thank you for the compassion you showed my mother and our family.

My mom was, simply, the greatest. I miss her every second of the day. If she could read this, I'd want her to know that I love her dearly and that my kids got all her best traits. Also, I floss daily now and go to the dermatologist once a year to get my moles checked, just the way she always told me to do. I hope she'd be proud.

About the Author

Kate Spencer is a writer whose work can be found in *Cosmopolitan*, *Rolling Stone*, the *Washington Post*, *Esquire*, *BuzzFeed*, *Refinery29*, VH1, *Women's Health*, *Salon*, *Scary Mommy*, and *Modern Loss*. She is a regular performer at the Upright Citizens Brigade Theatre in Los Angeles, where she lives with her family.